I.A.M.L. Guide

Figure 1. INTERIOR OF THE HASLINGER MUSIC SHOP IN VIENNA, c.1835.

INTERNATIONAL ASSOCIATION OF MUSIC LIBRARIES
Commission for Bibliographical Research

GUIDE FOR
Dating Early Published Music
A MANUAL OF BIBLIOGRAPHICAL PRACTICES

COMPILED BY
D.W. Krummel

JOSEPH BOONIN, INC.
Hackensack, New Jersey

BÄRENREITER VERLAG
Kassel · Basel · Tours · London

1974

TYPOGRAPHY AND COMPOSITION
Graphics Company · Urbana, Illinois

ISBN: 0-913574-25-2
Joseph Boonin, Inc. · Hackensack, New Jersey

ISBN: 3-7618-0465-2
Bärenreiter Verlag · Kassel · Basel · Tours · London

Library of Congress card no. 74-81916

Acknowledgments

Credit for the preparation of this text belongs to those persons who have attended the recent meetings of the International Association of Music Libraries in order to discuss music bibliography. As Compiler, my task has been largely one of organizing facts and reconciling viewpoints. I will concede to having pressed the case for several favorite interpretations (most notably the terminology in section I.D. of the Synopsis), perhaps more strongly than several respected colleagues were prepared to endorse without major reservations. The National Reports have also been heavily edited, partly for uniformity of style and partly to include several recent discoveries and writings. The study ought none the less to be viewed as a group effort.

This is as it should be. In music bibliography, research has developed under a benign spirit of respectful cooperation, probably more conspicuously so than in most other fields. Some of this can probably be explained by the scholars who have worked prominently in the field, notably librarians — especially cataloguers — motivated by various philosophies of "library service," as well as dealers and collectors, anxious to convey their enthusiasm with their favorite documents. Through their attitudes, a shared fascination with early printed music has developed. The documents with which we work are indeed the embodiment of many of our revered masterworks and so much of our musical heritage. But, meanwhile, they are too often marred by errors, confused by variant texts, and of uncertain usefulness for lack of such a basic amenity as a date. Thus our fascination becomes not only pleasant but also purposeful. Furthermore the quantity of printed music is immense, and none of us will ever be likely to master all of it bibliographically. We have all become specialists, but not without continuing to believe that our studies can benefit from the experience and encouragement of our fellow specialists. Whether all of the details of the early music printing and publishing practices — the complications and frustrations which we encounter as specialists — can be appropriately or usefully fitted into a systematic outline, such as I have attempted to do in the Synopsis, may be open to question. But such matters do need to be collected and described, since they contribute to the historic context in which any scholar must view his materials. Moreover, the treatment of details too often tends to be abbreviated, slanted or sacrificed altogether both in our massive projects for bibliographical control over early musical documents, such as RISM, and through the application of our IAML cataloguing rules. Thus our Commission has prepared this book, under my guidance.

In particular, I owe my special gratitude to the following: The American Philosophical Society, for a grant which enabled me to prepare the Synopsis in consultation with various European scholars; the American Council of Learned Societies, the Newberry Library, and the S.R. Shapiro Fund for other travel awards; the Research Board of the University of Illinois for various assistance; the most active members of the Commission, particularly Dan Fog, Cari Johansson, A. Hyatt King, François Lesure, Maria Prokopowicz, Alan Tyson, and Liesbeth Weinhold, who have given so much of their knowledge and time, especially in criticizing the Synopsis; the contributors of the National Reports; Hermann Baron, Rudolf Elvers, Richard MacNutt, Albi Rosenthal, and Claudio Sartori, for specific examples; Fredson Bowers, Frederick Hudson, Jan LaRue, and Jan Olof Rudén, for useful scholarly advice in their areas of special competence; Eric Greenfeldt, Larry Kroah, Kenneth Lavender, Marianne Kozlowski, and Rayna Baker for bibliographical searching and checking of the contents; Frank O. Williams for help with the design and layout; Mrs. Jane McClellan and Bernard E Wilson for editorial criticism of the final text; and the various libraries which provided photographic work, as identified in the List of Illustrations, among them particularly the Newberry Library.

D. W. Krummel
Urbana, March 1974

Contents

Preface

I. *Early Musical Editions*

Bibliography, which is the study of books as material objects,[1] has been mainly concerned with the type-set book containing a literary text. The present *Guide* is an attempt to apply the principles of bibliography to musical editions, particularly those issued between 1700 and 1860. As a method for music bibliography, this study is directed toward one of the first problems a scholar faces in working with musical documents: the assignment of a date of publication to those editions which typically bear none.

In what ways is music special among the various kinds of published material? Why has it come to be issued in its distinctive forms, which the bibliographer must treat in exceptional ways? First of all, its notation is more complicated, especially for the printer. It may be true that there are fewer basic shapes needed for the symbols than for a literary text: instead of the 26 letters of the alphabet, music requires only a few different indications of time duration. But the notes which we use must be placed on the staff lines, in vertical positions to represent the different pitch levels. For some kinds of music, several notes which sound simultaneously must appear in one vertical alignment. Furthermore, the staff itself must be printed. Sometimes the notes on the staff are also tied together, whether by slurs or by beams (ligatures). They may also be modified by other special signs indicating dynamics, pitch alteration, or articulation. By the 18th century, the problems in dealing with such notation were such as to require printers who specialized in music. Music publishers also became specialists, in response to an entirely different set of problems: The purchasers of music were generally fewer, more restricted in their

---

[1] W.W. Greg, "Bibliography — A Retrospect," in *The Bibliographical Society, 1892–1942: Studies in Retrospect* (London 1945), p. 25. The terms "scientific bibliography," "analytical bibliography," and "historical bibliography" are often used to distinguish the kind of study that is involved here, from the task of compiling lists of books ("descriptive bibliography"). Such inventive formulations as "bibliology" have not met with enthusiasm; nor has the term "musicography," which might be applied to the present work.

range of interests, more widely scattered, and probably less affluent than were the purchasers of printed books.

Soon after the invention of printing, music was also reproduced from movable type. Most music printing before 1700 used this method. Not until the early 18th century were modes of publishing developed which suited the peculiar needs of music. The new method of printing became the so-called "intaglio" process, using metal plates on which the lines, notes, and other printed marks were engraved. This process provided various advantages, slightly different ones for the printer than for the publisher. The printer was no longer committed to the simple linear sequence of symbols as in a literary text — letters, words, sentences, and paragraphs. The whole surface of the plate could be used to suit the demands of the notation. As for the publisher, he could keep the plates as long as he wished, running off copies as he needed them. With movable type, after a pre-determined number of copies were printed, the type was distributed. If more copies were required, the type had to be re-set. This was expensive. Engraved plates enabled a music publisher to work with a smaller investment, since paper was also very expensive. He could hope to make his living by paying for many insignificant failures with several lucrative successes.

In addition, engraved plates could be easily altered. A faulty passage could be corrected simply by pounding out the passage on the plate from behind and then re-engraving a new text. Thus the composer could (and sometimes did) change his mind about the content; or an editor could (and sometimes did) revise, add, or delete fingerings, musical markings, translations, and the like. New plates could also be substituted, in order to replace plates that either were worn out or needed many changes. Finally the publisher found himself with greater freedom in his commercial activities: he could (and very often did) change the price, issue excerpts from a larger work, combine plates in order to assemble an anthology, rearrange the order of works by re-numbering the plates, and advertise both other music he had for sale and places where copies could be obtained, and call attention to a new address for his shop.

The plates, engraved at one date, might be revised later; new plates could be substituted at an even later date; and the printing done even later. In contrast, early books were ordinarily printed as soon as the type was set, and published as soon as all of the printing was done. The imprint date in a typeset book is therefore likely to be a meaningful statement, whereas that on engraved music is probably not.

Yet for various reasons the scholar needs to know the date. The printer's and publisher's expedient thus becomes the scholar's puzzle; the assignment of a date becomes a highly problematical inquiry. We must go to the trouble of establishing facts which the printer and publisher, intentionally and for rather good reasons, chose to omit. As we shall see, we must at the outset decide exactly what the date does and does not mean (see the Synopsis, I.D.,E.). Later our study ranges afield to require a search for those various historical facts which may prove relevant to our immediate problem. Frequently, in return, the search for the date will uncover details, usually interesting and sometimes important concerning the work itself, its circumstances of publication, and its historical audience. As a result, dating has come today to be viewed as the central bibliographical research problem with music of the 18th and 19th centuries.

II. *The Need for Dating*

There is always much in history upon which we can rely, so long as we always remember that we are talking about documents and not events.[1]

Events that cannot be made to fit into some chronological scheme are scarcely ever material for the historian to handle. . . . An undated or undatable document is in most cases of no use to him.[2]

We can consider the significance of a particular musical document only after we have answered some very important questions. Was the creator of the text likely to have been able to approve or to correct the text as it came from the press? What is the relationship between this document and another one containing the same text, i.e., is one based on the other? Who might have used it and who could not possibly ever have used it? Such questions can be viewed at the outset as serving three different scholarly ends:

1. *Editorial Use: Textual Authenticity.* Dating is important in studying the content of a particular musical work. Editorial study seeks to establish the composer's original text; we often have no dependable holograph, or sometimes we may wish to confirm or even to correct the holograph. (We are, in fact, coming to discover that authentic editions often prove a better source than certain kinds of holographic material, in that they may incorporate the composer's final decisions on the content.) "If the history of our culture is ultimately the history of the writings of our great men," Fredson Bowers reminds us, "then we should have a passionate concern to make sure that we are reading them aright and not in corrupt texts that in hundreds of cumulatively important ways distort, blunt, obscure, modify, or contradict what in fact they were saying."[3]

---

[1] Morse Peckham, *Beyond the Tragic Vision* (New York 1962), p. 25.

[2] Gilbert J. Garraghan, *A Guide to Historical Method* (New York 1946), pp. 89, 194.

[3] *Bibliography & Modern Librarianship* (Berkeley, Los Angeles 1966), p. 25–6. "The works which relate to books," and serve man's noblest needs, according to Bacon, include "new editions of writers, with correcter impressions, more faultless versions, more useful commentaries, and more learned annotations" (*Advancement of Learning*, 1623, 1900 ed., p. 8).

12

The correct text is usually sought by editors for purposes of re-publication (as a so-called "Urtext" edition), and also by conscientious performers with a strong commitment to the composer's original intentions, as well as by musicologists for purposes of stylistic analysis. The task of determining authenticity ordinarily begins with an arrangement of the different versions, so as to establish their causal sequence. Given one particular version, what was it based on, and what other versions were based on it? The result is a *stemma*, which in its simplest forms grows out of the composer's manuscript. But frequently the picture is much more complicated than this: the composer made alterations to the earliest version after the first copies were printed; or he arranged for the simultaneous publication of two versions which themselves happened to be different, whether by design or by oversight. In any event, before such things can be determined, the different versions must be arranged chronologically, requiring a formulation of the dates. Only after dates are assigned can the editor consider the authenticity of the different versions, and their relation to each other.

2. *Bibliographical Use: The History of Documents.* Editions are also studied for their physical form, rather than for their musical content. This study involves not the text of a particular work, but the output of a particular printer or publisher. Dating is no less important in such a study than it is in editorial work: A firm's history can be written only after its practices have been identified and explained, which requires that individual editions be dated. In this case, the primary reason for dating is slightly different. The editor is interested in dating as a basis for rejecting those versions which are not authentic or germane to his study; whereas the bibliographer needs dates as evidence of the chronology of events. The practices of early publishers, as analyzed by modern scholars, thus become the basis for the methodology of studies such as the present one.

3. *Cataloguing.* The cataloguer dates music on general principles, for no specific immediate use. But, presumably scholars will some day consult the item, finding a date useful, even if it needs verification and perhaps revision. There may also be secondary uses for the cataloguer's dates, involving the internal operations of the library. In order to arrange all versions of the same work on the shelf chronologically, the date may be needed as part of the call number. The copy may be assigned to a special location because of its date (all publications before 1800, or 1820, or

13

1850, may be arbitrarily designated as "rare" and kept in a restricted area). Finally, procedures may be (indeed, should be) established for reporting all items to RISM[4] if their date is before 1801.

> NOTE: The antiquarian music dealer should be included in this category of users of dates. His importance in the history of the development of music bibliography cannot be overemphasized. The dealer establishes a date in order to describe accurately what he is selling, as a means of providing information which he is willing to stand behind. He may also discover something interesting or significant about the copy he is selling, thereby both enhancing the value of his copy and adding to the general store of our knowledge. During the 1930s, antiquarian dealers were among the first to be interested in dating as a subject of inquiry. Even today, the respected authorities in music bibliography include a significant number of antiquarian music dealers.

Such are the primary reasons for dating music. (Further comments on this point may be found in the Synopsis, I.C.). The differences among the three scholarly objectives must always be kept clearly in mind. If recent music bibliographers, for all their achievements, need to be faulted for one major shortcoming, it would probably be for their failure to accept the fact that different scholars have different goals. Thus the editor has sometimes been seen as a tiresome searcher for inconsequential minutiae, the bibliographer as working only "skin-deep," the cataloguer as doing a necessarily inferior job of dating that might better not be done at all. All three activities, however, are intellectually valid in their own right; and each is useful to the other two.

As a result of two generations of scholarship in matters of dating, a complicated task can now be performed with considerable precision and a minimum of effort. It is not inconceivable that some day the practice of dating might be abandoned, in deference to other kinds of information. For instance, we might be able to specify the exact relationship of the document in question to other copies of the same text (e.g., "2nd state, 4th issue, 1st edition"); or we might summarize or enumerate the bibliographical points of our copy (e.g., "lacking the opus number on the first page but with plate numbers, as in the A:Wn copy but not the F:Pc or I:Bc copies"). For now, the careful formulation of a date offers the most useful basis for the bibliographical study of early musical editions.

---

[4] i.e., the International Inventory of Musical Sources (*Répertoire internationale des sources musicales*), in large degree an updating of Robert Eitner's *Quellen-Lexikon*, undertaken by IAML and the International Musicological Society.

III. *Background & Plan*

The Commission for Bibliographical Research is the third name for one of the working commissions of the International Association of Music Libraries. At the 1959 meetings of the Association, a committee was proposed for the purpose of clarifying certain bibliographical terminology;[1] but apparently such a group was never organized. Four years later, the Plate Number Commission was established in order to compile a master index of plate numbers.[2] This activity led to the preliminary published list, "Cotages d'éditeurs antérieurs à c.1850."[3] At the meetings of the Association in 1966, the broader function of the group was reflected in a new name, the Commission for Dating Early Music. The activity started at this time has resulted in the present book. As this project has approached completion, the function of the group has seemed to call for a still more general name, the Commission for Bibliographical Research.

The present book consists of two parts. The Synopsis is a systematic outline of the methodology, which seeks to incorporate and organize the commonalities of bibliographical research. It was originally prepared by the Compiler, published,[4] circulated for comments to various scholars within the Commission and in related fields, discussed at the annual working sessions of the Commission in 1969 and 1970, and approved at the latter. The second part is a series of National Reports. Most of these were prepared by scholars who have specialized in the particular bibliographical areas in question, in response to an inquiry which was circulated in November 1968.

As a summary of the "state of the art" of dating early music, this

---

[1] Cecil Hopkinson, "Towards a Definition of Certain Terms in Musical Bibliography," in *Music, Libraries, and Instruments* (London 1961; Hinrichsen's 11th Music Book), p. 155.

[2] Various reports on the work of the Commission appear in *Fontes artis musicae,* 10 (1963), 4; 11 (1964), 140; 12 (1965), 82; 14 (1967), 65–6; 15 (1968), 39; 16 (1969), 17; 17 (1970), 37–8; 18 (1971), 70–1; 19 (1972), 189–90; and 20 (1973), 11.

[3] *Fontes artis musicae,* 14 (1967), 22–37.

[4] *Fontes artis musicae,* 18 (1971), 40–59.

book will be used by various readers in different ways. The scholar who specializes in musical documents has heretofore had very few "ground rules" in matters of methodology and terminology. Even assuming that there are three basically different uses for dating (those of the editor, bibliographer, and cataloguer), we are still faced with the many diverse practices of music publishing, in different areas and at different times. The specialist who works with British music published around 1740 has defined his subject and sees his needs in terms of his own experience, which is with the publishing practices of John Walsh. In many ways, Walsh's practices are unlike those of Artaria in Vienna in 1780, of Pleyel in Paris in 1820, or of Ditson in Boston in 1860. Devices which are useful in working with one are likely to be unimportant, sometimes even misleading in work with another. Music bibliography, as it develops in the years ahead, will need for its scholars to reach some general understandings in matters of procedure and terminology (hence the Synopsis); and it will need for them to benefit from the experience of their colleagues (hence the National Reports).

Furthermore, the scholar who concentrates in non-musical subjects may find that his study extends to the question of undated music. Political songs are interesting to the general historian, illustrated covers to the art historian, poetical settings to the literary historian, textual references to the social historian. Such researchers will usually need to begin with one of the National Reports, perhaps referring also to parts of the Synopsis. On the other hand, the beginner, who has never worked with undated music and expects to do a good deal of it, should first digest the brief Epitome which follows, and then proceed to the Synopsis. Meanwhile, let us remember, all of the rules, hints, warnings, and leads make very little lasting impression without copies with which to work. The examples described and shown in this book help to create a more realistic presentation; but bibliographical competence finally depends on the experience of working with original editions.

An outline structure has been used in most of this book for several reasons. Foreign users especially, it is hoped, will find its points easy to grasp. Also, examples can be considered distinctively. Since the field of music bibliography has never been the subject of a special survey and since it is continuing to expand at a very healthy (while not spectacular) rate, omissions and new findings can be incorporated into the total picture. At the same time, an outline structure tends to suggest a false assumption of proceeding from first principles. The bibliographer searching for information useful in dating is much like his next-door neighbor, the textual critic, the scholar whom A.E. Housman likened to the dog hunting for fleas: If the dog proceeded "on mathematical principles . . . he would never catch a flea, except by accident. . . . Every problem which presents itself . . . must be regarded as possibly unique."[1] Surely the scholar will waste much valuable time if he proceeds from point to point through the outline of the Synopsis as he examines each piece of music he is seeking to date. The outline structure, as a systematic overview of the findings of scholars working with all kinds of musical editions, is useful to the extent that it enables us to see our field in perspective, and to draw analogies for our work more easily.

The wide margins in this book are intended to invite annotation. Indeed, as a first study in its field, the present *Guide* is inevitably (I fear, despite the best efforts of several readers) filled with minor errors and omissions. Such annotations are often interesting and important enough to deserve separate publication. Even the minor additions and corrections, it is encouraged, should also be reported, either to the Compiler or to other active members of the IAML Commission for Bibliographical Research.

[1] *Proceedings of the Classical Association,* 18 (1922), 69.

Epitome

Basic Rules for Dating Music

These statements are intended to aid the beginner in work with undated musical editions. As such, their purpose is to summarize by outlining the most important methods, not to over-simplify by reducing the process of dating to an easy application of a few convenient principles. Indeed, the basic intent of the *Guide*, particularly the Synopsis, is to help the user to understand some of the various complications, ambiguities, and misrepresentations which are involved in dating. The references below will lead to the fuller discussions of some of these problems.

1. For the specific purpose of establishing a date, you should work first from the title page. When the text suggests one date and the title page suggests another, follow the title page. (See the Synopsis, I.D.2 and I.D.3.c.) There are some exceptions to this rule (as in the case of *Plattenauflagen*: see I.D.2.a.ii.), but these are very infrequent.

2. The pages of an edition or the title page often have plate numbers. You can often determine an approximate date from a chronology of the publisher's sequence of these numbers. (See the Synopsis, II.)

3. The publisher usually gives his address, almost always the city and often the street and number. Directories often tell you exactly when the publisher worked there. (See the Synopsis, III.)

4. Specific editions which were available from a publisher are frequently advertised in another of the publisher's editions. Sometimes an extensive catalogue is included. Known dates, either for the edition containing the notice or for the editions mentioned, will help you to establish the date for the edition at hand. (See the Synopsis, V.)

5. A work cannot have been published before it was composed. The first edition usually appeared about the time of the first performance, but there are many exceptions to this rule. (See the Synopsis, VII.A.)

6. If a copy bears a stamp of a dealer or the signature of an owner which can be dated, the edition must have appeared earlier. (See the Synopsis, VII.C.)

7. Hints of the date — either of when the music was composed or of when the edition was published — may be found in the visual appearance of the copy, the style of the music, references to specific events (whether in the text, in a dedication, or in an illustration), and often in the statement of the price. (See the Synopsis, VI., VII.D., and VII.E.)

8. Dates are often assigned in other bibliographies and catalogues. If you are absolutely sure that the copy being dated is exactly the same as the one described, and if you trust the compiler of the other work (which you should not do uncritically), use his date. (See the Synopsis, VII.G.)

9. Specialists and beginners alike are seldom so fortunate as to be absolutely certain that some later student will not improve upon their work. Err on the side of caution (i.e., use queries, circas, and other qualifying statements; and favor the later date over the earlier), and always tell what evidence you are using in assigning dates. (See the Synopsis, I.A., I.H.)

Synopsis

Figure 2. **A PARISIAN MUSIC SHOP IN 1782.** Engraving
by Louis Binet in Restif de la Bretonne, *Les Contemporains*
(Leipzig? 1782). According to the text, this Marcellinian
scene shows "La jolie-marchande-de-musique répondant à
l'exclamation de son mari, 'C'est votre mère'!"

I. *Introduction*

A. GENERAL ASSUMPTIONS. Ours is an age of intellectual cooperation. Recent scholarship has been characterized by large international projects, aided by modern technology and communication. Our achievements, however, have been possible mainly because scholars believe that research is done more authoritatively and, ultimately, more easily when they work together, each contributing his special knowledge and opinion. The differences between scholars — in languages, attitudes, and training — give us more comprehensive and more widely useful results. These differences, however, tend to make our projects more cumbersome and diffuse. It is useful therefore to begin this discussion by reminding ourselves of several painful and discouraging truths about bibliographical work:

1. Printers, engravers, and publishers did things differently from one another, and in different ways at different times in their careers, for purposes of meeting different and changing needs.

2. Printers, engravers, and publishers developed their practices in order to meet their own needs, not the needs of future scholars.

3. Everybody — engravers, printers, and publishers (as well as scholars), of yesterday, today, and tomorrow — makes mistakes. Not all mistakes are ever noticed or corrected; and correction is usually possible only through a statement in another publication, leaving the original error forever to mislead those who do not know about the correction.

Footnotes in the Synopsis are documented on pp. 112–6.

(A.) 4. It seems unlikely that we have now many of the final answers to our most important questions. (Perhaps we are not even asking the right questions.) The quantity of evidence from earlier periods remains relatively constant: a few discoveries are made while, unfortunately, a few documents are lost to us. In contrast, great advances have been made in the art of using and interpreting our evidence. Such progress inclines us to forget how subject we are to the changing perspectives (and limitations) contributed by our training, attitudes, and abilities.

B. THE SCOPE OF THIS STUDY. This book describes the means by which dates are assigned to music published between c.1700 and c.1860.

> NOTE: It is unfortunate that the reader must begin by accepting a logical flaw: How can one be sure that an edition comes from the period of this study, 1700–1860, unless one already knows the date? And if the date is already known, why use this book? Two important assumptions emerge from this predicament: (1) established dates often need to be verified and refined; (2) music from the period of this study can usually be dated at first sight in a very approximate way, through the composer's name, the visual characteristics, and the musical medium. Generally, the principles developed here also apply to music published before 1700 and after 1860.

1. With the development of a music publishing industry after 1700, which produced copies from engraved plates rather than from movable type, the serious problem begins. Since the plates could be stored easily, and copies could be made at any time, the statement of a date became, in a sense, inappropriate.

a. Engravings from all periods, whether of pictures, charts, maps, or music are often undated. Most engraved music before 1700 is also undated, but the quantity is not large. The dating problems either have already been solved or are unlikely to be solved through the use of the devices and sources discussed in this study.

b. Much of the music printed from movable type, the common method before 1700, carries a printed date, although that in particular from around 1800, using the new methods developed by Breitkopf and others, is seldom dated. Most of the music lithographs which first began to appear around 1800 are also undated. The procedures and sources discussed here will often be useful in dating such editions.

c. A large part of the music which was issued after 1860 remains undated; but the dating problem is different because of several factors. More bibliographical evidence is extant. Furthermore, publishers, in their willingness to accommodate scholarship and to serve a supposedly timeless rather than a rapidly changing audience, listed their new publications in journals and often in current bibliographies. And, new printing methods were developed. The terminal date of 1860 is admittedly arbitrary and unfortunate. A later date would have made this book much more useful, but would also have doubled, perhaps tripled the work, particularly in the National Reports.

2. The techniques discussed here should aid studies other than dating, most notably those concerned with textual authenticity (see I.C.2. below). In a sense, however, dating remains the critical process in the bibliographical study of printed music. In importance, it may be viewed as analogous to collation of a type-set book to the extent that once the scholar has investigated the matters involved in dating, the significance of a particular copy has probably become apparent.

3. Although this study is concerned with printed music, many of the devices and sources should prove useful in studying manuscript music.

C. THE USERS OF DATES.

The most accurate possible date (to recall the Preface) is needed, by different kinds of scholars:

1. *Bibliographers,* in their study of the documentary evidence of music — the history and practices of the men and firms who produced musical editions. Bibliographers make use both of the dates and the evidence which is used in establishing dates.

> NOTE: The most important statement of the bibliographer's point of view — perhaps stated a bit more controversially than would please many bibliographers, however — is Cecil Hopkinson's "Fundamentals of Music Bibliography," *Journal of Documentation,* 11 (1955), 119–29.

This category usually includes the "general" historian — specifically the scholar whose study depends on the evaluation of particular musical documents but does not concern itself primarily with the authenticity of the text. To the extent that he is concerned with dating the artifact (rather than the text), he functions as a bibliographer. But insofar as his resources may be delimited by the purposes of his inquiry, he resembles the cataloguer (discussed in 3. below).

(C.) 2. *Editors,* in their search for the composer's authentic text and its background; and performers and other scholars in their critical studies of the text. To the editor, dates are important in determining the authenticity of a text. This process in turn requires an establishment of the chronological sequence of the various versions.

EXAMPLES: Of the many instances which could be cited, the following may be regarded as typical:

1. In the first English edition of Handel's *Suites de pièces pour le clavecin,* the composer reports, "I have been obliged to publish some of the following lessons because surrepticious and incorrect copies of them had got abroad." In point of fact, there are new errors in this edition, corrected in manuscript on some of the copies, and on the plates in others.[1]

2. Regarding the recently celebrated instance of the quartets, op.3, by Haydn or by Hoffstetter, see Figure 3.

3. In the first edition of Beethoven's third symphony, measures 150—1 of the first movement are repeated. This repetition was deleted from later impressions. The fermata in measure 4 of the first movement of Beethoven's fifth symphony originally extended for one beat, but was changed by Beethoven to cover two.[2]

4. For an instance of a first edition which is preferable as a source to the autograph manuscript, see Alan Tyson, "Mozart's Piano Sonatas," *Musical Times,* 107 (1966), 888.

5. Regarding the two versions of Schumann's *Jugendalbum,* see II.C.2.b., Example 4 below.

6. Later states of the Kistner edition of Mendelssohn's cello sonatas contain Mendelssohn's own metronome markings, not found in earlier states.[3]

Significant changes, it can be proposed, are most likely to be found in major works, by scrupulous composers (like Beethoven), working with careless publishers (like Artaria).

3. *Cataloguers,* in their service to users of the copies which they describe. Included here are cataloguers working in libraries, cataloguers preparing lists for publication, and antiquarian booksellers. Their search for evidence which will bring out the importance of the items being described, for a potential user or purchaser, has added much to our knowledge of dating. The goal of the cataloguer is to serve all likely users, including bibliographers and editors. At the same time the cataloguer, working under pressures of time and faced with a wide range of

Figure 3. **BIBLIOGRAPHICAL EVIDENCE IMPORTANT IN THE STUDY OF TEXT.** The "Opus 3" quartets were long attributed to Joseph Haydn because his name appears on the title page of the early editions. Recent scholars, however, have questioned the attribution, mostly on grounds of style. Furthermore, although no copies of the earliest state are known, it can now be seen that the plates originally attributed the music to "Hoffstetter." His name was deleted, probably in order to use a more famous name to sell copies; and other publishers, copying this edition, repeated the faulty information. See Alan Tyson & H.C. Robbins Landon, "Who Composed Haydn's Op.3?" *Musical Times*, 105 (1964), 506–7; also Hubert Unverricht, *Die beiden Hoffstetter* (Mainz 1968; Beiträge zur Mittelrheinischen Musikgeschichte, 10), pp. 54–7.

Figure 4. **A COMPOSER'S CORRECTIONS OF PROOF.** A page of the proof sheets of the Brandus edition (Paris 1848) of Meyerbeer's *Le Prophète*.

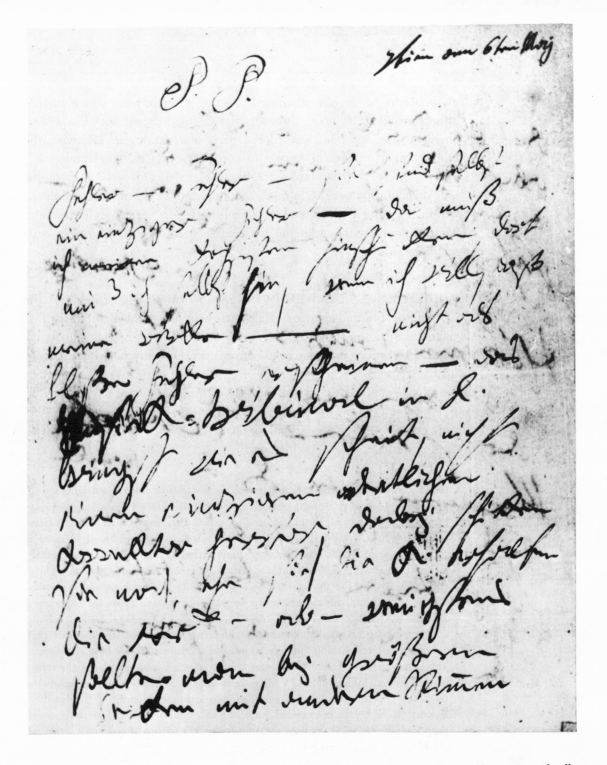

Figure 5. "Mistakes – mistakes – you yourself are a unique mistake" ("Fehler – Fehler – Sie sind selbst ein einziger Fehler"). So begins this letter from Beethoven to his publisher. It serves to suggest, perhaps a bit unkindly but not too strongly, the critical attitude needed by the editor (also the performer) in his work with early published music. "You will see," Beethoven remarks later in the letter, "that the piano arrangement of the Egmont overture is lacking a whole measure." See Anderson, I, 320, also Kinsky & Halm, p. 231.

(C.3.) materials to be described, must learn the point beyond which further efforts are likely to prove unproductive or inconsistent with the general character and intended use of the particular catalogue. Likewise, the bibliographer and editor must also accept the fact that the cataloguer's dates may be undependable, not because the cataloguer was incompetent or lazy, but because a more accurate date could not be established within the time allowed, and because libraries do not generally consider it appropriate to re-catalogue their early materials in the interests of scholarship.

D. DIFFERENCES BETWEEN COPIES. We now come to one of the most complicated and controversial matters in any field of bibliography, involving the basic relationships among various copies of the same work which display minor differences in content. In the study of printed books, standard terminology has been developed. The definitive (if not quite universally accepted) discussion of this terminology appears in Fredson Bowers, *Principles of Bibliographical Description* (Princeton 1949), beginning pp. 39–42. These standard terms may be adapted for use with musical editions in the following way:

> NOTE: Music bibliographers disagree as to whether or not the terminology of general bibliography, growing out of experience with literary texts, mostly printed from movable type, should be used for musical editions, mostly printed from engraved plates.[4] Inevitably there are disadvantages and problems in using a system of terms which was developed for a different kind of material. Furthermore, there is some heated (but respectful) disagreement among general bibliographers regarding the use of their own terms, both in principles and in details. On the other hand, advantages are to be gained from drawing on the experience and the systematic thinking of several generations of general bibliographers, concerned with essentially the same problems. It is also well to remember that no system of terminology unique to musical editions has ever been developed. The present study therefore endorses the use in music bibliography of the terms of the general bibliographer. Various refinements of bibliographical technique are often applicable to musical editions, and a thorough study of treatises like Bowers' is highly recommended for the music bibliographer. For the present purposes of this book, however, a fairly general and superficial explanation of the basic concepts seems best and safest.

1. An *edition* consists of the whole number of copies printed from substantially the same printing surfaces (be they settings of type, engraved plates, or lithographic stones), at any time or times.

NOTE: The important qualifying word "substantially" is discussed in I.D.5.d. below.

2.   An *issue* consists of "the whole number of copies of an edition put on sale at any time or times as a consciously planned unit." In the case of a re-issue, some planned and externally visible indication of a change in publishing arrangements must be in evidence. Any change constituting a true re-issue, therefore, must always have occurred after public sale of the first form, or original issue, had commenced; moreover, re-issue ideally implies the withdrawal of the previous issue from sale (quoted and paraphrased from Bowers, p. 40).

> EXAMPLE: Mozart's *Sonates pour le clavecin,* K.6–7, were first issued "Aux adresses ordinaires" in Paris in 1764. The plates were later taken to London, and re-issued with a new title page devised by Leopold Mozart. A third issue appeared around 1765 when the plates became the property of the London publisher, Robert Bremner.[5]   See also Figures 6–11.

a.   The title page is critical in determining the issue. Alteration of the imprint information on this page, whether by replacement of the page or by re-striking or adapting the plate, is the basis for a new issue.

> See Figures 12–13 for an example of a new plate which repeats the same information. Such changes presumably are not in themselves sufficient to result in a new issue, although the point may be debated.

i.   Cancellation of a title page, often seen in books printed from movable type, is rarely seen in printed music. Since press runs from engraved plates were usually small, there were few copies in need of changing, and for these manuscript alteration or paste-over imprint labels (see VII.E.3.c. below) were generally sufficient. Perhaps it was also reasoned that the mounting of a completely new leaf would result in the weakening of the physical copy, which needed to be extremely durable for heavy use by performers.

ii.   Therefore most re-issues of music are the result of a new printing of copies rather than an adapting of unsold copies, as is so often true of type-set books. A copy of music with a new title page is ofter referred to in music bibliography with the German term *Titelauflage.*

NOTE: Some disagreement exists among German scholars, however, as to

(D.2.a.ii.) what precisely is meant by this term. To some, a new publisher must be involved; to others, only the original publisher may be involved (otherwise the result is a new edition); and to still others, a *Titelauflage* results from any new title page (even if no changes in publishing circumstances may be involved, as in Figures 12–13).

For a rare instance of a *Plattenauflage,* see I.D.5.d. below, Example 9.

b. When an edition identified only by a caption title (at the head of the first page of music) is supplemented by a wholly new and complete title page, a new issue is the result. Similarly, when a number of small editions are brought together and re-issued with one collective title page (as with an opera score assembled from the separate editions of its individual selections), the item is a re-issue because of the collective title page. Such title pages, however, must not be confused with wrappers (see VI.D.6 below), which are generally on paper quite different from the paper used in the main text, and, if present, generally occur when there is a full title page (but not when there is only a caption title). (See I.D.7. below)

c. In dating it is essential for the bibliographer and cataloguer to distinguish various issues (and to the extent that they work from title pages, this is the logical and easy thing to do). Nevertheless, this distinction may prove quite irrelevant to the editor, since the musical text itself may be completely unchanged.

3. The term *state* (or *variant*) can be applied to any form of musical publication which exhibits variations in content caused by purposeful alteration of the printing surface.

a. Engraved plates were very easily altered by re-striking. New plates were often substituted for worn or faulty ones. This might have been done any time after the plates were first prepared and before they were destroyed. Furthermore, the publisher who made such changes was, of course, under no obligation to mention the changes, and in fact usually found it inconvenient and even undesirable to do so.

b. Since alteration of the content may have resulted from the composer's specific instructions, the editor in search of an authentic text must study *all* copies which make up an authentic edition to locate variant states. Fortunately, he can eliminate those editions which are clearly not authentic, as well as certain issues and states of authentic

32

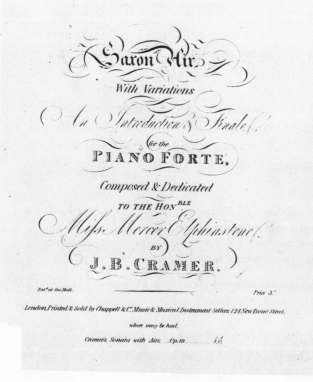

ISSUES AND STATES OF AN EARLY ENGLISH PIANO WORK. *Figure 6 (upper left):* The original Chappell edition, entered at Stationers Hall on 4 March 1811. *Figure 7 (lower first):* The imprint statement of the second Chappell state, which now mentions other music of Cramer. *Figure 8 (lower second):* Same as Figure 7, with the Chappell imprint now covered by Mitchell's paste-over label, which can be dated c.1811–1821. *Figure 9 (bottom):* New issue by Latour, with the imprint altered. Latour was a partner in the Chappell firm until 1826. Thereafter he operated his own firm which presumably acquired the rights to the plates for this work from Chappell. In 1830 his firm was absorbed by Chappell. *Figures 10 & 11 (upper right):* "Textual" variants on the first page of music. The changes were made between the first and second states. Similar changes were made on the second page, but apparently nowhere else. Cf. Figure 106.

London, Printed & Sold by Chappell & Cº Music & Musical Instrument Sellers, 124 New Bond Street,

where may be had

Cramer's Sonata with Airs   Op. 19   1.6

& all the Works of the above Author.

Sold at **MITCHELL'S** Musical Library & Instrument Warehouse, 159 New Bond Street, opposite Clifford Street,

where may be had

Cramer's Sonata with Airs   Op. 19   1.6

& all the Works of the above Author.

London, Printed & Sold by F. T. LATOUR Music & Musical Instrument Seller, 50 New Bond Street,

where may be had

Cramer's Sonata with Airs   Op. 19   1.6

& all the Works of the above Author.

(D.3.b.) editions in which any possible changes could not possibly be authentic. Today his task is facilitated by mechanical collation and by convenient access to distant copies via photography.

c. The cataloguer, on the other hand, should ordinarily be satisfied in establishing the date of the issue, regrettably disregarding the different states, known or likely, unless these different states are described in an authoritative, readily available source and are themselves datable.

> NOTE: It is frequently difficult to differentiate between a new state and a new issue. By definition, a new issue is re-issued: its conditions of publication are changed. A new state contains a different text. For further discussion of this very complicated matter, however, see I.D.5. below.

> EXAMPLES: For evidence of different states, see Figures 10–11, 14–19, and 125–6 below.

d. Alterations in ink may have been made by the publisher, often at the request of the composer. If this can be established, new states are involved. For instance, three states exist for certain Breitkopf & Härtel editions of Mendelssohn's *Lieder ohne Worte*.[3] Some have errors uncorrected, some have errors corrected in ink, while some have errors corrected later by changes on the plates. The authenticity of the corrections, and their dates, can sometimes be established through correspondence between composer and publisher (see VII.C. below).

4. The term *impression* describes all of the copies as a unit run off the press at one particular time (i.e., as one "press run").

a. The existence of different impressions can be determined from several kinds of evidence.

i. *Different lots of paper.* In principle, such evidence is highly problematical. Strictly speaking, a printer could have used several kinds of paper in one press run. In times of paper shortage, as Thomas Cross must have experienced around 1695,[6] this probably did happen. Unfortunately, it also seems likely that music printers, like book printers, put together sheets and gatherings from various press runs to fill out partial copies. (If terms may be devised for this situation, we would say that many copies which appear to be "integral" are in fact "hybrid.") Even so, it seems safe to consider most instances of new lots of paper, including the examples cited below, as reasonably conclusive for purposes of detecting the existence of two or more impressions.

EXAMPLES:

1. The two extant copies of the fourth Walsh "edition" [sic] of Handel's *Messiah* are different only in that the chain lines run in different directions.[7]

2. The extant copies of the Clementi edition of John Field's *Sonatas,* opus 1, are known to have at least four different watermarks — dated 1800, 1801, 1802, and 1812. A fifth copy has an undated watermark. The exact date of publication can be found in an announcement on 25 March 1801.[8]

3. James Power in London brought out the numbers of Thomas Moore's *Irish Melodies,* a popular work which went through many impressions, with watermarks which are dated between 1808 and 1829.[9]

ii. *Damaged and worn plates.* Wear was caused by rubbing the plates dry after the inking and by cleaning after the impression of copies, but *not,* as is usually believed, by the heavy pressure of the rolling press. Soft plates (pewter or lead) wear out more quickly than hard ones (copper or zinc), but were preferred for work with music because they were more easily incised. Wear is evidenced by cracks in the plate; and the cracks are usually progressive: the uncracked form is earlier than the cracked one, and the slightly cracked form earlier than the badly cracked one. The darkness of the copy, on the other hand, is likely to be evidence mostly of the inking of one particular copy, and not of a whole press run. Cracked plates are characteristic of early Viennese editions, probably because of a special alloy used there in making the plates. The statement is often made that plates began to deteriorate after the impression of 1,000 copies: the original source of this information, however, has not been cited in recent literature, and the figure seems rather high.

For examples of cracked plates, see Figures 14, 17, and especially 177 below.

iii. *The presence of a list of subscribers.* (See VII.D. below.) The presence of such a list is evidence of an early press run. The

(D.4.a.iii) absence of a list, on the other hand, may be evidence of a later press run; or it may be the result of the subscriber list having been lost.

iv. *Imposition.* In some instances, the arrangement of the plates in relation to the sheets enables us to distinguish two separate impressions.

> EXAMPLE: *The Battle of the Wabash,* an early American "Anacreon parody," was first published by Blake in Philadelphia, probably soon after the battle on 7 November 1811. The first impression contains four pages, the outer two blank and the inner two printed from two plates. The second state contains the text, "To Anacreon in Heaven," added above the staves of the voice part. The third state contains a third page of text with the text "Fort McHenry, or The Star Spangled Banner," and mentions a performance by Mr. Harding which can be dated 19 October 1814. This third state exists in two impressions, one with the first page blank and the other with the last page blank. Although Wolfe implies that the second of these came first, the opposite seems more likely. Presumably Blake had a stock of the sheets for the second state above (which, incidentally, is not extant in its "original" altered form). He is likely to have wanted to use them up before beginning a new press run. The use of partially complete copies from stock would also enable him to get copies before the public more quickly.[10]

b. It is axiomatic that two copies from the same impression display no differences at all in text. Therefore, the editor working with a particular text may use one copy as properly as another, provided that he has established that both come from the same impression. (The work of the editor would be much simpler if it were possible to establish this identity more often.)

c. The question of how many copies were usually run off in one press run is an interesting one. But, as Deutsch has observed, "while publishers of books are very proud to announce a new edition and the number of copies printed, music publishers on the contrary are too modest. . . . New editions are rarely indicated, the number of the editions [i.e., *Auflagen?*] hardly ever, and the number of copies never. . . . It is the custom to strike off the number of copies immediately required but whether these numbers are small or large is the publisher's secret."[11] Not only is the evidence scarce; but that which does exist unfortunately shows a wide range of practice. Without engraved plates, which offered the publisher an alternative to

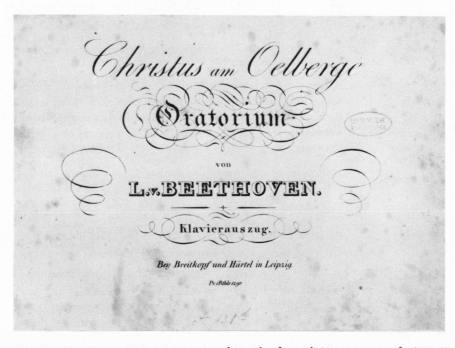

TITLE-PAGE IMITATION. *Figure 12 (top)* is from the first edition, typeset, of 1811; *Figure 13 (bottom)* is from the later edition, lithographed, of 1821. By working from title-page transcriptions, the careful user may notice the single difference (in the imprint, "&" and "und"). The second title page is obviously copied from the first, although the shading of the composer's name and the decorative curves below "Oratorium" are distinctly different.

(D.4.c.) standing type, it is doubtful that music publishing as it existed in the 18th and 19th centuries could have developed. While this technological refinement was a blessing to the publisher in that it allowed him to be more speculative, it is a curse to the scholar in that it ultimately required the publisher to be more secretive. Fortunately, we do have some scattered evidence of the size of particular press runs, such as the following:

> 200 copies in the first impression by Thomas Cross of Nicolò Cosimi, *Sonate de camera,* op.1 (London 1702).[12]

> Ordinarily about 100 copies in the first impression, later 20 or 50 for early German and Viennese editions.[13]

> 100 copies for the first impression by Breitkopf & Härtel of each of Beethoven's two op.70 piano trios (Leipzig 1809). For the fifth symphony (also Leipzig 1809), 700 copies were printed by Breitkopf & Härtel in seven different impressions before 1828, and 350 copies more in various impressions before 1862.[14]

> 600 copies of the Breitkopf & Härtel edition of Beethoven's *Arietten,* op.82 (1811).[15]

> 25, 50, or at most 100 copies in the early 19th-century editions of Friedrich Hofmeister in Leipzig.[16]

> A total of 446 copies in 22 different impressions, for the Schott edition of Kreutzer's *Lodoiska* overture, first published in Mainz in 1802. The impressions were for as few as one or as many as fifty copies; six of the impressions were fewer than seven copies. The 22 impressions cover a time span of eighteen years.[17]

> 100 copies of the first impressions of Grieg's opus 1 and 2, according to the C.F. Peters press books.[18]

5. The four terms describe ideal relationships, and are subject to numerous, diverse, and important variations in practice. In bibliographical description, such variations should be explained as completely as possible; terminology is a possible convenience, not an essential categorization.

a. In the abstract, the following distinctions may be useful:
     The concept of an *edition* reflects an integrity of *form;*
          that is, copies have in common their *general presentation.*
     The concept of an *issue* reflects an integrity of *commerce;*
          that is, copies have in common their *conditions of sale.*

> The concept of a *state* reflects an integrity of *content;*
> that is, copies have in common their *specific presentation.*
> The concept of an *impression* reflects an integrity of *production;*
> that is, copies have in common their *circumstances of printing.*

b.   The four terms are hierarchic. Their relationship can be shown through the specific example of the Artaria edition of the piano arrangement of the overture to Mozart's *Zauberflöte.* (Illustrations of this edition are shown as Figures 14–19.) The sequence of the copies is as follows:

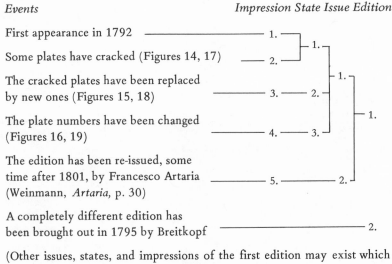

(Other issues, states, and impressions of the first edition may exist which are not extant or have not been identified.)

Several matters mentioned above can be illustrated by this example. First, there is no convenient way to date the states and impressions of the first issue, other than to say that they appeared between 1792 and 1801. And, second, the content of the first three states (judging from the two pages shown) is identical, except for some minor notational changes which were probably determined by the engraver.

c.   This example is quite simple compared to the one drawn up by Cecil Hopkinson: see "Towards a Definition of Certain Terms in Musical Bibliography," in *Music, Libraries, and Instruments* (1961), p. 148. While Hopkinson's example is hypothetical, each of the circumstances it describes might very easily be encountered by the scholar. The guidelines suggested in this study would appear to call

PLATE DETERIORATION, RE-PLACEMENT, AND EMENDA-TION: the Artaria edition of the piano arrangement of Mozart's *Zauberflöte* overture (Vienna 1792). The original plates may be seen in *Figure 14 (top)* to have developed serious cracks. New plates were engraved, as seen in *Figure 15 (center)*, with the same plate number but some notational changes, mainly in the last line. (Such notational changes, it can be seen, are neither truly accidental nor truly substantive.) In the third state, seen in *Figure 16 (bottom)*, for some reason the plate number was deleted.

Figures 17–19, showing the same three copies as at left. It will be seen that the tempo markings are calligraphic on the original plates, but punched on the replacements. Above all, compare the plate numbers for these replacement plates with those at left. In Figure 18, the number 377 has been deleted.

(D.5.c.) for the following designations (the numbers refer to Hopkinson's example):

2. Addition of a plate number	= new state
3. Addition of a catalogue conjugate with the music	= new state
4. Re-engraving of three page of music	= new state (see d. below)
5.,7.,13.,19. Title-page references changed	= new issue
6. Expansion of the catalogue	= new state
8.,9.,15.,20.,22. New prices, engraved	= new issue
10. Removal of the catalogue	= new state
11.,12.,17. New street addresses	= new issue
14. New prices, in ink	= new issue
16.,21. New publisher	= new issue
18. New engraved title	= new issue or state
23. New lithographed text	= new edition

d. Given two copies which have the same title page, but numerous changes of or in the plates, we must formulate some arbitrary rules for distinguishing new editions from new states. (A similar distinction is often needed between editions and issues.) The following suggestions are advanced, subject to later discussion and refinement:

i. A new edition results when 20 per cent. of the plates in the earlier of two copies, both of about the same length, are replaced or substantially altered in the later copy.

ii. A new edition results when 30 per cent. of the plates in the longer of two copies (which may be either the earlier or the later) are deleted, replaced, or substantially changed for the shorter one.

iii. A new edition results when changes in content, of any extent, can be identified with a particular known performance.

iv. Re-numbering of pages, or the addition or deletion of plate numbers, should not be regarded as significant alteration.

v. Cataloguers, lacking copies to compare, should assume that a copy in hand is the same as one described in a bibliographical citation of another copy. As a general rule, two obviously different copies reflect different states or issues until there are specific grounds for assignment as a different edition.

EXAMPLES: 1. Of two Parisian copies of the score of Piccinni, *Atys,* copy 1, published c.1780 by the composer, contains 332 pages; while copy 2, published c.1790 by Des Lauriers, also has 332 pages, but with 171 new plates. The instrumental parts are re-orchestrated, apparently with only minor changes, although the editor would need to determine such importance. In this instance, the second copy should be considered a new edition rather than a new issue.[19]

2. Of two copies of the score of Gluck, *Alcestis,* copy 1 contains 305 pages, while copy 2 contains 293 pages, of which 278 are the same as in copy 1 (some are re-numbered), 27 pages of the earlier copy having been conflated into 15 of the latter copy. In this instance, the second copy should be considered merely a new state, not a new edition.[20]

3. Of two copies of the score of Grétry, *Les deux avares* (Paris 1770?), copy 1 contains 134 pages. Copy 2 contains 155 pages, of which 128 are the same as in copy 1, 6 of the earlier having been replaced by 17 in the later. In this instance, the second copy is a new state.[21]

4. There are three copies of the Naderman score (1791) of Cherubini, *Lodoiska.* Copy 1 contains 410 pages, also a five-leaf supplement with a separate title on p. [1], music on pp. 2–9, and the last page blank. (The separate title suggests that the supplement was conceived separately, as an addition to the existing work.) Copy 2 contains 410 pages, but also has a 16-page supplement between pp. 119 and 120 (the verso of 119 and the recto of 120 are blank), as well as the same five-leaf supplement as in copy 1, which however lacks the separate title on p. [1]. (This lack of the separate title suggests that the supplement was now part of the whole.) Copy 3 contains 434 pages, numbered continuously and including both of the supplements. In this instance, copies 2 and 3 are new states.[22]

5. Of three copies of the Farrenc full score of Beethoven's *Fidelio,* copy 1, in three acts, has a price of 80 fr., and an address of "Boulevard Poissonnière No.22." Copy 2, also in three acts, has a price of 125 fr., and an address of "Rue St. Marc, No.21," but is otherwise identical with copy 1. Copy 3 is identical with copy 2 in price and address, also in the rest of the content, except that the opera is now in two acts. In this instance, copy 2 is a new issue; copy 3 is a new state, at least until such time as its relationship to specific events in the evolution of the opera from its three-act to its two-act form can be determined. From the evidence of the publisher's address, it would appear that this sequence is correct, although Kinsky-Halm has reversed the three.[23] Copy 1 dates from 1826, copies 2 and 3 from the 1830's.

6. There are two copies of the second edition of Lully's *Roland.* Copy 1 contains 233 pages and is dated 1709. Copy 2 contains 4 + 233 pages and mentions on its title page a performance on 15 December 1716. In this instance, copy 2 is a new edition (see I.D.5.d.iii. above).[24]

43

(D.5.d.Ex.6.)   7. Of two copies of the 1859 Choudens piano-vocal score of Gounod's *Faust,* copy 1 contains 224 pages. Copy 2 has the same title page, but with the phrase added, "2e Édition avec les Récitatifs Ajoutés par l'Auteur." Although only about 30 pages have been changed or altered in copy 2, the changes are significant, and the designation as a new edition seems appropriate.[25]

8. There are two copies of the Walsh edition (1707) of the pasticcio, *Thomyris.* Copy 1 is unpaged, without the overture, and the title page corrected in ink. (Advertised on 26–29 April 1707.) Copy 2 is paginated, with the overture and the title-page corrections on the plate. (Advertised on 17–19 June 1707.) In this instance, copy 2 would be best designated as a new edition.[26]

9. A famous curiosity is the Cappi edition (1802) of the Beethoven piano sonata, op.26, an example of what Deutsch has called a "Plattenauflage" (in contrast to a "Titelauflage"). Copy 1 has the words "Composé et dedié" on the title page, as well as an address of "Place St. Michel No.5" and a price of 1f.40. Copy 2 has the same title page, but altered with words "Composée et dediée," the address "Place St. Michel No.4" and a price of 2f. Since the title-page plates are so nearly identical, one might suspect that two issues are involved. The music itself, however, has been completely re-engraved. (In effect, the normal pattern of bibliographic cancellation is reversed: one saves the title page and replaces the rest of the book.) This is certainly evidence of a new edition.[27]

10. Less famous but no less curious is the instance of two copies of the Walsh score of the opera *Ezio* (London 1755). Copy 1 identifies the composer as Perez; copy 2 identifies the composer as Hasse. Since the content is apparently otherwise identical (a case of saving the music but replacing the composer), the second can hardly be viewed as any more than a different state.[28]

11. Three or more states are involved in the Cluer edition of Handel's *Suites de Pieces pour le Clavecin,* Volume 1.[29]

12. Cracked plates were replaced in the Artaria edition (1784) of Mozart's sonatas, K.330–2.[30] The British Museum copy contains 23 of the original plates and 15 new ones: obviously it must be considered a new edition, different from the one which appeared in 1784. But at what point does|the latest new state become different enough from the original to become a new edition? Can there be any more intelligent solution to this problem than the arbitrary rule advanced above (I.D.5.d.)? See also Figures 14–19.

13. Another instance of replacement of a single plate is seen in Figures 125–6. (In this case, the later state can be dated through the plate number.)

14. The first edition of Clérambault's first book of *Pièces de clavecin* carries the date 1702. The plates were later corrected, new pages added — along with a privilege dated 1704 — and the date on the title page changed to 1703, clearly producing a new edition.[31]

f. The following translations appear to be appropriate:

English	*French*	*German*
Edition	Édition	Ausgabe
Issue	Publication (or Émission)	Auflage
State	État (or Variant)	Variant
Impression	Tirage	Abzug (or Abdruck)

The French translations have been formulated in Roger Laufer, "Pour une description scientifique du livre en tant qu'objet matériel," *Australian Journal of French Studies,* 3 (1966), 252; and Wallace Kirsop, *Bibliographie matérielle et critique textuelle* (Paris 1970), p. 32n. The term "issue" poses the most serious problems. Renouard proposed using *tirage,* although this places an inappropriate emphasis on the work of the printer. Several booksellers, such as Georges Heilbrun, have preferred *émission,* which seems acceptable.[32]

The German translations are beset by the widespread use of the terms *Ausgabe* and *Auflage,* which have clear connotations and a well defined relationship to each other. Unfortunately, the connotations and the interrelationship are slightly different from what we require. The act of publishing (literally, of "giving out") is conveyed by *Ausgabe,* the act of printing (literally, of "setting up") by *Auflage.* Thus the relationship becomes, in a sense, nearly the opposite of that which we are seeking: *Ausgabe* means something closer to issue, *Auflage* to edition or perhaps even to impression (as when, for instance, Kinsky-Halm, p. 214, speaks of "15 Auflagen" before 1864 of Beethoven's C-minor *Fantasie,* op.80). The current general practice, however, is to accept *Ausgabe* as edition, and to recognize a hierarchic relationship between *Ausgabe* and *Auflage* (one *Ausgabe* usually consists of one or more *Auflagen*). Furthermore, the term *Titelauflage,* used so widely with early music, refers clearly to a kind of issue, specifically one which is distinguished by a replaced (or cancelled) title page.

In all three languages, the terms for impression are used to designate a single copy which comes from the press, as well as the group of copies which results from a single "press run."

6. The copy itself, meanwhile, comprises two slightly different entities:

a. It extends to include only those sheets essential to (i.) the identi-

(D.6.a.) fication of the publication, and (ii.) the presentation of the text. In other words, the title page and the music make up the edition, although the subscriber lists, tipped-in illustrations, and supplementary text — if present — could also be considered part of the basic text. But wrappers, added publishers' catalogues not conjugate to the title page or text, and other material superfluous to the content and the publishing event are not an essential part of the copy.

b. It extends to include whatever was known or likely to have been offered for sale in the earliest copy (see I.E.1.c. below), including wrappers, catalogues, and the like.

c. The second definition would appear on general principles to be the better one to follow, especially when bibliographical sophistication is needed. Often, however, the precise entity is impossible to determine.

> **EXAMPLE:** The libretto may, or may not, be seen as an integral part of the Breitkopf & Härtel full score (1801) of Mozart's *Don Giovanni*.[33]

7. Having discussed bibliographical items which are essentially integral in their texts, we must turn briefly to those items which are composite in their texts. Among the common kinds which one encounters in work with musical editions are series collections, copies with supplements, and "made-up" copies.

a. The title page ought to be trustworthy; if dating as a routine library activity is involved, the title page should be presumed to be correct. For instance, we may know that a title page for a series collection bears the date of the first number, but that the last number probably appeared at a much later, undetermined date. Under such circumstances, the busy cataloguer should be satisfied with the title page, although the editor and bibliographer will want to look further.

b. In the case of a book with a supplement, the title page may need to be overlooked. The appearance of the supplement results in a re-issue: in effect, the original edition as such was presumably withdrawn from sale, and henceforth sold only with the supplement attached. Sometimes the title page was altered to mention this fact; but with such information lacking, it is usually not possible to tell whether the original item was acquired first and the supplement later, or whether the two were acquired at the same time. Under the first circumstance, we would have two bibliographical items with two different dates, while under the second circumstance we would have one item dating from the time of the re-issue. In the absence of any evidence in favor of the former, it would appear safer to presume the latter circumstance.

c. Opera vocal scores were often collected from sheet-music excerpts (Philip Gossett calls this a "layer" plan). In the absence of evidence to the contrary, we should presume that the excerpts were issued first, although there may be late impressions of the excerpts which postdate some impressions of the collected vocal score.

d. The use of plates for individual selections in more than one anthology was rather common at certain periods. The British Museum's Hirsch IV.192,[34] for instance, is a *Zauberflöte* collected vocal score which begins with the Artaria overture (discussed above and shown as Figures 14–19) and continues with vocal selections taken from a *Sammlung von Arien* collection. Such re-use, like that mentioned in c. above, is often reflected in multiple pagination (see VI.E.4. below).

e. There are extant copies of anthologies which have a title page in manuscript or, sometimes, an engraved passe-partout title page with the significant text entirely in manuscript.[35] In working with such books, it is important to ask — and usually impossible to determine — whether the publisher collected the sheets and sold them as a unit, or whether the anthology was put together by or for an owner. In the absence of evidence to the contrary, one should presume the latter, especially if the graphic evidence of the different parts suggests the workmanship of several different engravers.

f. Unfortunately, there seem to be some music books which were conceived with the special intention of individualized assembly for a particular purchaser, much like certain early engraved atlases. Some late 18th-century provincial English and American religious instruction music books come to mind. Description of one copy of such a book for bibliographical purposes should be undertaken with a view to facilitating, if possible, the detailed collation of the copy in hand with another copy assembled from the same basic "repertory" of plates.

(D.) 8. In addition to the terms edition, issue, state, and impression, it is useful — especially for the needs of the editor — to accept into usage the concept of *version*. One version differs from another in content; the changes may be major or minor. Different versions may be manifest in different editions or states, but rarely in different issues. A classic example of important differences in version, as reflected in various bibliographical ways, is Wagner's *Tannhäuser*.[36]

E. THE MEANING OF THE DATE.

E. THE MEANING OF THE DATE. The date is understood to be the publication date, i.e., the time when copies were first placed on sale to the public, in the form specified.

> NOTE: In the process of issuing an edition there are many steps, each with its significance. Among these events are the date of composition, the date of the engraving (often the most impressive in that it is the earliest, and hence the favorite among owners), the date of the composer's approval of the text as it appears on the plates (obviously the crucial one for the editor), the date of the latest emendation of the plates (also extremely important), the date of copyright, the date of announcement, and the date of the press run. All these events cannot possibly have taken place on the same day. Nor is the sequence of steps necessarily the same in each history of an edition. Furthermore, we usually consider ourselves fortunate to know any one of the above dates.

1. A publication date applies to an edition.

   a. Later issues and variants are also dated from the first placement of copies on sale to the public (although correctly speaking, only an edition is "published;" an issue is "issued," a state is "produced," etc.).

   b. For various reasons, some music was never intended to be sold, having been printed for private distribution or for rental use. Ideally, such copies should be dated from the presentation by the owner to the first recipient; practically, it is often easier to think in terms of the date when the printer delivered the copies to the owner of the edition.

   c. In the discussion which follows, the term "earliest copy" is used to refer to a hypothetical copy which was printed as part of the first impression and offered for sale on the very day of publication.

   > NOTE: The concept of "earliest copy" may be seen as a counterpart to the general bibliographer's concept of "ideal copy" (see Bowers, pp. 113–23).

Just as "ideal copy" is based on a study of relationships of physical form, reflected in descriptions (particularly collation formulas), so "earliest copy" is based on a study of relationships of time, reflected in dating.

2.   It is often useful to make a distinction between a copy date and a publication date. The former is the date of the latest possible issue (or, when it can be dated, the state) which is evidenced in a particular copy. The latter is the date of the first appearance of an edition, such as will be announced in other sources. The difference may be seen in two questions: What is the date of my copy of the Artaria edition of Mozart's *Zauberflöte* overture? And, when did Artaria first publish its edition of this music?

a.   An extant copy may vary from the earliest copy in issue or state. Different impressions are presumed to be irrelevant for dating purposes.

b.   A publication date may safely be presumed to be the copy date, and vice versa, only after the extant copy has been proven to be identical with the earliest copy. This can be done only through a collation of the extant copy with another extant copy known to be identical with the earliest copy.

c.   For practical purposes, and with an element of risk accepted, the extant copy may be presumed to be the same as the earliest copy when:

i.)   the music itself appears to have been so unimportant in the years following its publication as never to have required a second impression of copies; and

ii.)   the extant copy is plausible in its bibliographical appearance as an example of the earliest copy, and shows no evidence of alteration of the plates.

3.   The bibliographer's task is one first of establishing the publication date, then if necessary, of establishing the dates of particular copies. On the other hand, the editor's concern in dating involves a painstaking and scrupulous search for any possible way in which the extant copies may differ from the earliest copy, i.e., the publication date may differ from the copy date. Although the cataloguer is concerned mainly with the dating of copies, he usually accepts a publication date in the absence of

49

(E.3.) any specific and reliable evidence that the extant copy with which he is working proves unlike the earliest copy — and the better the cataloguer, the more likely he is to be aware of any such evidence.

F. KINDS OF DATES. Different evidence helps in various ways to identify a publication or a copy date, by producing the following kinds of dates:

1. A *terminus post quem,* or the earliest possible date. The date of composition is a *terminus post quem* for the first edition, which in turn in a *terminus post quem* for all later impressions, states, issues, and editions.

2. A *terminus ante quem,* or the latest possible date.

> **NOTE:** Alternative Latin formulations are sometimes seen. The *terminus a quo* (from which) is the same as the *terminus post quem* (after which), while the *terminus ad quem* (to which) is the same as the *terminus ante quem* (before which).

3. Inclusive dates, i.e., a *terminus post quem* on one side and a *terminus ante quem* on the other.

4. Relative dates, apart from specific years and dates. For instance, the editor's interest usually consists in knowing which of two copies is earlier. How much earlier, or the exact dates of either are not important.

5. Approximate dates, generally understood to include a span of five to nine years, and by implication favoring a date near the middle of the span.

6. Probable date, subject either to doubt or to an error of a year on either side.

7. Exact date, varying in precision according to the needs of the user. The cataloguer is ordinarily satisfied with an exact year; the bibliographer and editor sometimes need to devote their efforts to establishing a month and date.

G. CONVENTIONS IN STATEMENT. The bibliographer and the editor can and should express the date as fully and as precisely as possible. The cataloguer, on the other hand, must accept certain conventions in abbreviation.

1. The rules for assignment of dates are specified in section 3.45 of the International Association of Music Libraries' *Rules for Full Cataloging,* compiled by Virginia Cunningham (Frankfurt 1971; Code International de catalogage de la musique, III.), pp. 46–7. Among these rules, the following are appropriate to the present discussion:

a. "When the date is not on the title page, supply it from elsewhere in the work or from bibliographical sources. If date of publication cannot be determined, date of printing, of legal deposit, or of copyright may be substituted."

b. "If the date of publication as given on the work is known to be incorrect, add 'i.e.' and the correct date within square brackets."

c. "Dates may be approximated as follows:

[1892 or 3]	one of two years certain
[1892?]	probable date
[ca.1892]	approximate date
[bet.1749–1752]	approximate date
[189–]	decade certain
[189–?]	decade uncertain
[18––]	decade unknown"

2. In practice, the following accommodations to the cataloguing *Rules* appear to be appropriate:

a. Dates established exclusively from plate numbers are probable, not certain.

b. Dates derived from a publisher's address are usually inclusive dates, and can be stated as approximate dates using "bet." ("between," or in some libraries, "inter").

c. Unfortunately, there is no provision in the *Rules* for terminus dates (i.e., "pre-1801" or "post-1772"). The cataloguer must thus decide whether to find a complementary terminal date (i.e., instead of "pre-1801," use "bet.1794–1801"), or to use another kind of approximation (i.e., instead of "post-1772," use "c.1770" or "176–?").

d. In some catalogues (such as Squire's of the British Museum), an approximate date was generally stated as *circa* the nearest year ending in 0 or 5 (i.e., "c.1745" instead of "174–").

H. PRESENTATION OF EVIDENCE. The dating of music is becoming more exact and more reliable. Furthermore, ours is an age of cooperative research and international bibliographical control. For such reasons, it is particularly important that any date which is established — by an editor, a bibliographer, or a cataloguer — should be supported by a statement, specifying briefly or implying clearly what evidence was used to establish the date.

II. *Plate Numbers*

A. THE BASIC PRINCIPLE. Many publishers (sometimes their engravers) assigned numbers to their publications, beginning with number 1 for the earliest and proceeding upwards in order. The range of these numbers can be correlated with particular years, through various other kinds of evidence. When the existence of such a correlation can be established, dates can be derived from the plate numbers. In other words, plate numbers give us what might be called a "parachronology."

> **EXAMPLE:** As a simple and randomly selected instance, André editions with plate numbers 270 and 280 are known to have come from 1789. An edition with plate number 275 probably also dates from that year.

1. The reliability of a plate-number date is increased by the quantity of adjacent numbers which have been dated; and is diminished by the deviant dates found among the adjacent numbers, as well as by the remote numbers which interfere with the basic sequence.

> **EXAMPLE:** *The Oliver Ditson Catalogue, 1845–1850, as a Case Study.* In practice, the bibliographer generally groups the numbers he accumulates in three categories: those which clearly fit a given year, those which overlap the numbers from an adjacent year, and those which clearly do not fit the year. On the basis of the first of these, the basic parachronology is established. The second of these usually can be accounted for by the fact that plate numbers were not assigned at the exact time of publication, or at the exact time of the evidence in question. As an example, the plate numbers of the Boston publisher Ditson for six years

53

(A.1.Ex.) can be roughly assigned (through copyright depository copies in the Library of Congress) as follows:

Year	Clear assignment	Overlap	Contradiction
1845:	1011 26 40 48 49 50 51 57 76		10 1257
1846:	1080 86 95 97 98 99	1215 1237	
	1116 21 35 39 46 91		
1847:	1240 42 44 46 47	1211	1092
	1250 51 59 62 66 68 75 79 82 84 91 94 95 96		
	1300 01 09 10 11 14 16 19 23 32 38 39 40 45 46	1449	
	1351 54 60 62 79 84 90 91 92 95 96 98 99		
	1402 06 07 10 13 14 18 19 20 21 22 26 27 28 29		
	1430 31 32 33 34		
1848:	1454 58 66 68 70 72 80 84 85 91 95	1439	377 1729
	1505 21 22 24 25 27 28 32 33 34 36 37 39 40 41	1637 1651	
	1542 43 44 45 46 47 48 49 53 56 58 60 61 66 67		
	1568 70 71 72 73 74 76 77 79 81 82 83 84 86 87		
	1588 89 90 91 98 99		
	1605 07 08 09 10 11 15 21 24 25 27 31		
1849:	1660 61 62 63 66 67 68 69 71 73 74 85 86	1636 43 49	
	1713 39 47 57 61 77 78 79 84 86 87 91 94 96	1820 30	
1850:	1811 13 14 16 17 28 36 37 40 45 57 59 60 64 67	1795	
	1874 76 78 80 81 82 84 85 90 91 92 93 97		
	1907 10 13 40 52 66		
	2118 46 50 56 58 59 67 86 88		
1851:	2236		

The numbers between 1211 and 1237 were probably assigned toward the end of 1845, and some of the editions with these numbers were actually issued in 1845 while others did not appear until the next year. The same is probably true of numbers 1439–49 in the next year, of 1636–51 in the year after, and perhaps of 1795–1830 in the following year. In explaining the outright contradictions, on the other hand, several conjectures are possible. The number 10 may not be a plate number at all; 377 may have been planned by a different publisher, who sold the plates, with his number on them, to Ditson; 1257 and 1729 were perhaps delayed in publication, the contract having been signed and the title page registered, but the engraving not completed and the plate number not assigned until several years later. In contrast, 1092 was probably engraved and the number assigned in 1846, but for some reason the work was neither copyrighted nor issued until the next year.

One further wonders what happened to the numbers between 2000 and 2099. Through such examination of the music publisher's catalogue, a simple beginning can be made toward a bibliographical study of his whole production. Plate numbers provide an exceedingly arbitrary view of this production, at once both highly attractive and highly deceptive because of the simplicity of the integers. Until we are fortunate enough to be able to peruse the editions themselves (even photocopies of them), arranged according to the sequence of these integers, the integers themselves must be used for whatever they may or may not tell us.[37]

2. Plate numbers served originally to organize the plates of the publisher or engraver. Their precise functions could be several. The numbers no doubt helped to simplify the communication between publisher, engraver, and printer, and to arrange the work of each. These numbers were a useful means of keeping all of the plates and the sheets together during production, after which the plates were presumably stored in the warehouse in sequence according to the numbers. They may also have been used for the storage of the copies which had been printed, or for the publisher's inventory, perhaps even for ordering purposes. The accuracy of the numbers for purposes of dating, and their importance in the history of the engraver or publisher, are in direct proportion to our knowledge of such arrangements. Therefore, dates derived from plate numbers should usually be regarded as probable rather than exact: their statement should typically be qualified with a query.

3. Dated and systematically arranged lists of plate numbers are found in three kinds of sources:

a. Separately published lists, of which the most important is Otto Erich Deutsch, *Musikverlagsnummern* (Berlin 1961), covering mostly German publishers.

b. Other lists. Some thematic catalogues and bibliographies cite plate numbers and have special indexes of them. Several publishers' catalogues, such as the Bote & Bock *Vollständiges Verzeichnis* (1914), list the plate numbers for all of the works they contain.

c. Unpublished files, frequently maintained on cards in research libraries during the 1930s and 1940s, and currently being set up by individual scholars for their special studies. (A number of the card files from American libraries, which were not being maintained and were rarely used, have now been collected by the Compiler. These are available for reference consultation.)

4. By definition, plate numbers should apply only to engraved editions. Similar numbers, however, appear frequently in lithographed

(A.4.) music, and occasionally even in type-set music. The term plate number should be used generically as applicable to all of them.

B. PLACEMENT AND FUNCTION.   These vary from printer to printer, often according to regional practices.

1. The plate number usually appears near the imprint on the title page (as in Figure 86) and in the lower margin of each page of music, usually in the center (as in Figures 4, 15, and others).

    a. Sometimes the number is located in one of the four corners of the page of music, usually a bottom corner, left (as in Figures 81 and 117) or right (as in Figures 82, 84, 85, 134, and 144–6). Appearing thus, it can be confused with a page number.

    b. In editions in which two pages were printed from one plate, such as the "Parisian format" opera scores of c.1850, the number will usually appear in the bottom inner margin, divided between two conjugate leaves and partly concealed because of the tightness of the binding (as in Figures 113 and 116).

2. A number of publishers, particularly the early 19th-century Parisians, made a practice of preceding the plate number with the initials of the firm (as in Figures 4, 80, 109–12, 160, 173, 176, and 178).

3. In the mid-19th century, the plate number was often followed by another number, which appeared in parentheses or was separated from the plate number by a hyphen or dash. (See Figure 149, for instance.) The second number might indicate either the total number of plates of music, or a subdivision of a larger series.[38]

4. In English-language common usage today, the term plate number refers to all numbers used primarily in the printing, as distinguishable from the publishing, process.

    a. At one time an attempt was made to distinguish plate numbers from publisher's numbers. Plate numbers were unique to one plate, with successive numbers being assigned to each of the plates which made up an edition (i.e., plate number 250 might appear on the title page, 251 on the first page of music, 267 on the 17th page, &c.). In contrast, a publisher's number was one number which appeared on all of the plates which made up the edition. The latter is much more common. In any event, this basic distinction has now been forgotten.

 i. In German practice, *Plattennummern* are often distinguished from *Verlagsnummern.* Generally, the latter appears on the title page, the former in the music. Complicated rules governing terminology were established, and debated, in order to distinguish all possible circumstances; but these now seem to be in the process of being forgotten.

 ii. The French term *cotage* applies to all such numbers.

b. After 1850, plate numbers must be distinguished from edition numbers. The latter are a publisher's means of calling attention to particular editions, through special advertising and distribution, uniformity in design, and other forms of production and promotion.

 i. Edition numbers function much like series numbers, and can be indistinguishable from them. Such difference as ought to be made between the two involves the emphasis of the name: edition numbers almost always mention the publisher (i.e., "Edizione Ricordi," or "Schirmer's Library of Musical Classics," or "Edition Litolff") while series numbers usually call attention to a particular subject or medium (i.e., the "Kammersonaten" series of Breitkopf & Härtel or "Nagels Musik Archiv"). Regarding "Edition format," see VI.B.6.a. below.

 ii. Sometimes plate numbers are derived from edition or series numbers, or are specifically assigned to them, thus falling into a special sequence apart from the main plate number sequence.

 iii. An edition number was generally applied to a particular musical work, so that the same edition number would likely appear in what to the bibliographer would be entirely different "editions" of (i.e., the impressions from entirely new plates for) the same musical work.

C. LIMITATIONS OF PRECISION. Before plate number dates can be accepted as exact or even probable, several common pitfalls must be

(C.) avoided, i.e., the following questions regarding their functions must be answered:

1. When were the numbers assigned? In theory, the numbers do not comprise an absolutely reliable indication of the publication date unless they were assigned at the very time of publication. Such a convenience is in fact next to impossible, since the processes of engraving, running off of copies, assembly of sheets, and distribution each take time in themselves. Usually the numbers were assigned much earlier (i.e., when the edition was first being planned); or, occasionally, later. Sometimes, for instance, plates were unnumbered in the first (or early) impression(s), then numbered as they went to storage or as they were reprinted. When this happened, the plate number appears only on the later impressions, which thus become variant states.

> EXAMPLES: 1. Many Walsh editions were given plate numbers some time around 1730. Earlier states, lacking the plate number, exist for many of the numbered editions. The numbers are listed in Walsh's *Cattalogue of Musicke* of c.1740.[39]
>
> 2. Most, perhaps all, music printed by Allyn Bacon in Philadelphia, 1814–1820, appeared first without a plate number. The numbers were probably assigned when the plates went into storage after the first impression; so presumably the copies with the plate numbers represent later impressions.[40]
>
> 3. The Catelin edition of Berlioz, *Les nuits d'été*, op.7, appears in two states. In the first, the plate number 872 appears only on the title page; in the second, the number appears on all pages.[41]
>
> 4. When the Berlin firm of Schlesinger moved in 1823, the initial "S" was added to the numbers of all of the plates. Early editions can be distinguished from later publications, which all have plate numbers with the initials "A.S."[42]

> NOTE: In this matter, it is well to review two recommendations made previously: that the date should be assigned to a specific issue but not to a state, unless the state is itself datable (I.D.3.c.); and that the addition of a plate number is evidence of a new state but not of a new issue (I.D.5.c.). The implications are clear but the implementation can be complicated. For a Walsh edition which was advertised in 1724, with a plate number which was apparently assigned c.1730, is the date 1724 or c.1730? Smith would argue for a date of c.1730, which seems acceptable because the state can be dated, however approximately. For a Bacon edition of 1817 to which a plate number had been added, on the other hand, the date of 1817 would need to suffice, because we have no way of knowing whether the number was added immediately after the first impression, or several years later. Good arguments

can be made against both of these assignments, and the two assumptions made above may each be questioned, especially the second. (Why not consider the second Bacon edition a new issue, and formulate an "artificial date" such as c.1818. so as to indicate a difference from the 1817 copy?)

2. What are the inconsistencies in numbering, and how can they be explained?

a. It is not uncommon to find the same number on two completely different editions of the same publisher.

EXAMPLES:

1. Richault's plate number 11607 is seen in two editions of music by Hector Berlioz, the piano-vocal score of *La damnation de Faust,* and the piano-solo score of *La fuite en Égypte.*[43]

2. J.M. Götz in Mannheim used plate number 102 twice, in 1784 for Cambini's string trios, opus 5, and in 1791 for Haydn's clavier trios, Hoboken XV:16, 15. The same practice is seen in editions of Hummel, Schott, and Simrock.[44]

b. Several publishers issued completely new editions of one work with the same number as that used for previous editions. Presumably the number served as a location device: the new plates and/or copies were stored in the same location as the old ones.

EXAMPLES:

1. Beethoven's piano sonata, op.27, no.1, was issued in 1802 by Simrock, with the plate number 233. The same number appears on the edition from the 1850s, "revue, corrigée, métronomisée et doigtée par Ch. Czerny."[45]

2. For Beethoven's piano sonata, op.109, Schlesinger in Berlin used the plate number 1088 for two editions, an oblong one in 1821 and an upright one in 1835. (In the latter, the number reads S.1088.A, which is important in determining the lateness: See II.C.1., Example 4 above.)[46]

3. "Choudens, seventy-three years after their publication of the first edition of Bizet's *Carmen,* are still using the same plate number for the current edition."[47]

4. Breitkopf & Härtel used the plate number 6016 for two editions, with somewhat different texts, of Schumann's *Kinderszenen.*[48]

5. André plate number 4964 appears on three different versions of Mozart's *Eine kleine Nachtmusik,* K.525.[49]

c. There are many miscellaneous inconsistencies, a few of which have ingenious explanations. Sometimes a publisher ended one se-

(C.2.c.) quence and jumped to a higher number (e.g., Ditson 2000–2099 in the example cited in II.A.1. above). The new number may indicate that the plates were made by a different workman, produced under special auspices, or stored in a different area. Sometimes special numbers were reserved for particular composers; and at least one known sequence is alphabetical by title. Sometimes several series were maintained at once. It seems hardly likely that any series are truly random (i.e., assigned from a Table of Random Numbers); yet, for present purposes, this sometimes appears to be the case.

EXAMPLES:

1. Artaria presumably published the music of Gyrowetz very soon after it was first composed. Yet Weinmann reports the following sequence:[50]

> for op.1–9, the plate numbers 176–472, dated 1789–1794
> for op.10–15, the plate numbers 522–652, dated 1795–1796
> for op.16–21, the plate numbers 662–734, dated 1796–1798
> for op.22, the plate number 492, *dated 1794?*

2. One well-known gap in Ricordi numbers[51] dates from 1890, extends from around numbers 62600 to 94000, and has never been explained. There may be a similar gap in Lucca numbers soon after 1840, involving numbers between 6500 and 10000, and perhaps coinciding with a change from the use of oblong to upright format.

3. Breitkopf maintained different series for engravings, lithographs, and typographic editions.[52] Schott maintained two series in 1793, as did Imbault in 1797.[53]

4. Sieber's series of "Symphonies periodiques" had reached 26 numbers in 1788. These appeared first without plate numbers, but were later assigned numbers 42–62. Hereafter the plate numbers for this series jumped immediately to 1033, 1035, and 1036, ending in 1801 with plate number 1578 assigned to series number 53.[54]

5. In Dr. Arnold's edition of the works of Handel, the plate numbers are what Coopersmith calls "Bogen" (gathering) numbers. Each group of 48 pages has a separate consecutive number; within a gathering particular works may end and others begin.[55]

6. A publisher of a pirated edition might take the plate number from the edition which he was copying. For instance, J.J. Hummel's new engravings of the Tartini violin sonatas, op.1 and 2, bear the numbers 576 and 594, which are taken from the Le Cène editions which they copied.[56]

7. Addison & Hodson numbers follow no identifiable chronology.[57]

8. Although Pacini numbers are also apparently not chronological, he did keep together the Field piano concertos, but numbered them backwards, i.e.,

Concerto No.1, 445; No.2, 443; No.3, 442; No.4, 441; No.5, 440; No.6, 439.[58]

9. For a brief time, Hummel numbers apparently run generally backwards, i.e.: 70–83 = 1768; 82–92 = 1767; 94–99 = 1766. Between 1770 and 1805 the numbers generally appear to have been assigned in blocks, two sequences of numbers going on at one time.[59]

10. Pleyel reserved low plate numbers for his friends, according to Mrs Benton. "Wessel is known to have set aside a series of numbers for use on the works of a particular composer."[60]

11. The Philadelphia publisher John Aitken assigned numbers alphabetically by title rather than chronologically, i.e., A = 1–8; B = 9–18; C = 26–9; D = 31–6,&c. The reason why such an arrangement might be desirable is easy to imagine. But *how* it was done is quite another matter: How was Aitken to know that he would never publish more than ten works beginning with B?[61]

d. Often one publisher purchased plates from another. Sometimes the old numbers were retained; sometimes they were replaced; sometimes they were adapted by adding prefixes or suffixes. The presence of the publisher's initials helps sometimes to identify such re-issues.

EXAMPLES:

1. Many plates used by Carli in Paris were engraved by Richault. These all have a prefix "R" in their numbers.[62]

2. Falter issued three Haydn minuets with plate numbers 1, 2, and 3. In 1818, Schott re-issued them, adding a digit "1" to each number to produce 11, 12, and 13.[63] The same practice is seen in copies of the Leduc edition of Haydn's "3 Quatuors" (i.e., the Symphonies no.90–92, Hoboken I:166, 170, 173), in which the plate number 9 has been altered to become 189.[64]

3. Artaria acquired the plates of Torricella and reprinted them, adding his own plate numbers 118–47.[65]

4. Much more complicated is the case of the Hoffmeister plates taken over by the Chemische Druckerey.[66] The left column shows the original Hoffmeister numbers, the right the new number of the Chemische Druckerey:

1 = 291	303 = 303	325 = 325	A.W. = 388
2 = 292	306 = 306	326 = 326	208 = 389
3 = 293	30 = 308	327 = 327	op.14 = 391
58 = 295	11 = 311	340 = 340	185 = 392
332 = 298	12 = 312	33 = 341	188 = 393
29 = 299	13 = 313	324 = 382	91, 113,
300 = 300	14 = 314	323 = 384	129, 151, 152
301 = 301	15 = 315	325 = 385	(6 quintets) = 398
302 = 302	324 = 324	235 = 387	no pl. no. = 402

(C.2.d.Ex.) 5. Usually one publisher acquired such plates *en bloc*, sometime after the music had first been printed. Maurice Schlesinger, for instance, issued other Parisian publishers' music, selectively and soon after the music had first appeared, by leasing plates from such firms as Troupenas, Boieldieu, and Janet et Cotelle. These he altered so as to bear his own plate numbers.[67]

6. The existence of an earlier issue can often be postulated from plate numbers. A case in point concerns Berlioz' *Symphonie Fantastique,* in the Witzendorf edition. On the basis of the Witzendorf plate number chronology, the edition has been dated 1842.[68] But Witzendorf's edition is a re-issue, based on Trentsensky plates. Thanks to the work of Alexander Weinmann, we now know that the Trentsensky plate number 2824 should be dated 1836 — and indeed there is an announcement for this music from that date —, also that the Witzendorf edition in question should be dated from April 1844, when Witzendorf acquired the firm of Trentsensky & Vieweg.[69]

e. Sometimes a large publisher prepared the plates for a small or new publisher. Since the plates have the numbers of the large publisher, it was presumably he who retained control of the plates and ran off later impressions as they were needed.

EXAMPLE: Large firms in the United States, mainly those in cities, often published music for small firms, often for small-town music dealers. Firth and Hall in New York, for instance, used their own plate numbers 3984 and 4059–60 on music for P. Dickerson in Syracuse, New York (1846–1847); 3974 on music for D. Woodruff in Tuscaloosa, Alabama (1846); and 4218 on music for James W. Andrews in Troy, New York (1848). C.G. Christman in New York used his own plate number 52 on the music which he printed for J. Hjousbery in Brooklyn in 1846.[70]

f. Several publishers, especially from 19th-century England, used "plate title annotations" instead of plate numbers. These consisted of a brief, often abbreviated, statement identifying either the specific work or a publisher's series. These annotations could be helpful to the printer and publisher in immediately identifying plates or printed sheets, without recourse to an index of the plate numbers. Similarly, they can be useful to scholars today when they appear on extant copies which lack a title page. But for dating purposes their information is rarely useful. (Title annotations may be seen in Figures 73–4, 77, 87, and 112; series annotations appear in Figures 81 and 90.)

g. Other symbols sometimes appear in the position of a plate number, looking much like the mysterious "press marks" in printed books. The significance of these symbols can usually be determined, if at all, only through an examination of the entire output of the publisher. Initials (as in Figure 52) are seen often, miscellaneous signs (as in Figure 102) somewhat less frequently.

h. "Passe partout" title pages often present special plate number problems of their own. One decorative plate may bear the plate number of the earliest edition on which it was used, a plate number all its own, or – probably most frequently – no plate number at all.

j. Substituted plates are sometimes re-numbered, sometimes not. Altered plates are seldom re-numbered. Occasionally the most distinctive evidence of an altered or replaced plate will be the plate number not found in the earlier states. See Figures 14–19, 125–6.

3. Numbers which fall between the dated numbers of adjacent years can be assigned only by guesswork.

> **EXAMPLE:** *The Early Simrock Catalogue As a Case Study.* By examining plate numbers, we can often get some impression of the changing activity of a publisher. We must begin with some large assumptions which we know are rarely true: that all of the publisher's editions have plate numbers, and that the numbers are always chronological. Even allowing for the average margin of error in such matters, however, an analysis of the numbers can give us some useful information.
>
> The point can be illustrated through a study of the catalogue of Simrock in Bonn between 1793 and 1808, based on Deutsch's *Musikverlagsnummern.* In the chart below, the first pair of figures gives the dated plate numbers for each year, and the total number of publications which are therefore known to have appeared in that year (i.e., the range from the lowest to the highest of these numbers). The second pair of figures gives a literal projection, in which the undated numbers between any two years are assigned, the first half to the earlier year and the second half to the later year. Such figures probably distort the picture: the numbers which we know and have dated may all come from early or late in the year. The third pair of figures therefore is a corrected projection which attempts, in an approximate way, to adjust the series. In view of the accumulation of numbers in 1805 and 1806, for instance, it seems plausible that the single dated number for 1804 comes near the end of that year's sequence. (It seems a very small point to argue whether number 405 dates from late 1804 or early 1805; yet the cataloguer, in applying the principles of dating according to plate numbers, will need to choose, and the scholar will often need to guess.)

(C.3.Ex.)   **SIMROCK PLATE NUMBERS**

| | I. | | II. | | III. | |
| | *Evidence (Deutsch)* | | *Literal projection* | | *Corrected projection* | |
	Numbers	Range	Numbers	Range	Numbers	Range
1793	4	1	1—8	8	1—7	7
1794	13—15	3	9—19	11	8—16	9
1795	—	0	20—23	4	17—25	9
1796	27—28	2	24—32	9	26—35	10
1797	37—53	17	33—63	31	36—53	18
1798	75	1	64—84	21	54—75	22
1799	94—99	6	85—102	18	76—100	25
1800	104—130	27	103—133	31	101—130	30
1801	136—151	16	134—155	22	131—160	30
1802	161—242	82	156—263	108	161—250	90
1803	284—345	62	264—362	99	251—345	95
1804	399	1	363—411	49	346—400	55
1805	422—444	23	412—448	37	401—450	50
1806	452—501	50	449—522	74	451—510	60
1807	543—545	3	523—562	40	511—580	70
1808	581—643	63	563—650	88	581—650	70

While guesswork is the most we can expect from such figures, the tabulations are none the less useful, especially for the bibliographer attempting to reconstruct the history of the firm. Despite the minor differences between the literal and the corrected projection, both are in agreement on the general picture: that 1797 saw a new level of production established; that 1802 and 1803 were the best years of all; and that there was a sudden decline in 1804 (in part for political reasons involving the French occupation of Bonn, no doubt). It is possible that 1804 and 1807 were lean years, as the extant evidence conveys. But in this instance the corrected projection, which shows a more even production each year, may actually be closer to the truth than the literal projection.

4. The reliability of a plate number for dating purposes, depends entirely on the publisher in question. As a general rule, German numbers are thought to be more useful than French. (The plate numbers of Troupenas in Paris, however, are very reliable, while those of Schott in Mainz, according to Mrs Meyer-Baer, are not.)

For further information on plate numbers, see the National Reports below, item D.

III. *Publisher's Addresses*

A. SOURCES. The activity of a publisher at a particular street address provides inclusive dates for those copies which bear that address. The addresses may be located in several kinds of sources:

1. Contemporary directories, of cities or of trades. These have been used in preparing the modern scholarly directories below, and should be known to the editor and the bibliographer for purposes of of verifying and qualifying specific facts.

2. Modern scholarly directories, prepared in part from the contemporary directories and other related sources.

> NOTE: The one single important international directory of early music publishers is Robert Eitner, *Buch- und Musikalien-Händler* ... (Leipzig 1904), drawn from the *Quellen-Lexikon,* now out of date and usually without addresses.

3. Modern histories of early music firms, including Festschriften on the anniversary of the founding of a firm, and studies of the relationship between a composer and the publisher or transcripts of their correspondence.

B. EXACT INFORMATION. In matters of doubt or of great importance, it is often useful to determine exactly when a publisher moved. The directories may be misleading. For instance, they may fail to notice the fact that a publisher has moved, repeating the former address for several years after the move. In the other direction, let us imagine the hypothetical example of an 1821 directory compiled in October 1820, listing a publisher who moved in November 1820.

C. FORM OF IMPRINT STATEMENT. The form of the name used by a publisher in his editions can often be shown to be distinctive to a certain period in his career.

65

EXAMPLES:

1. The importance of the smallest details is seen in M.A. Guenin's duos, op.3. There are two entirely different editions involved (i.e., the plates are entirely different), although the music appears to be the same in both. Both were engraved by Mme. Annereau and published "by the composer." In the earlier form, the street address reads, "rue St. Honore;" in the second, "rue St. Honnore."[71] See also Figures 12–13.

2. Sometimes the directories are at fault. Boiëldieu was at 92, rue de Richelieu in Paris from 1820 to 1824. From the directories for these years, the address is given variously as 192, 292, and 32, almost surely all mistakes for 92.[72]

3. George E. Blake in Philadelphia used distinctive forms of his street address and the name of his business. Between 1802 and 1806 he referred to his "Musical Repository." In 1813 and 1814 he seldom used any street address at all. Between 1814 and 1817 he gave his street address as "13 South 5h. Street." Thereafter the form "5th." was more common.[73]

4. Peculiarities of German title-page forms around 1800 have been studied by Matthäus and Weinhold. In the 1790s, the common form of imprint is *A (A, In)* [place], *chez (bey, presso)* [publisher] (e.g., "A Offenbach chez Andre"). In the decade following, the preposition was usually omitted; the city and name of the publisher were reversed; and capitals were used more often.

5. Evidence of incorporation is sometimes useful. Before 1777, Johann Michael Götz in Mannheim used only his full name. After 1777, he used "Götz & Comp."

6. An instance (one of several) of a publisher being at one address too long a period of time for that fact to be useful in dating is the case of Lucca in Milan, who worked at the same address from 1825–1888.

7. Often the evidence of a street address conflicts with other evidence. Imbault's "Nouvelle Édition" of the Mozart quartets, with plate numbers 905, 906, and 910, has a street address of 200 Rue St. Honoré, which dates them before 1806. But this edition mentions the new Artaria edition, which did not appear until 1807 or 1808.[74]

D.   AGENTS.   Often a publisher arranged for other publishers or dealers to distribute his editions. The addresses of such agents, and the periods of time when the two were working together, may prove useful in dating.

EXAMPLES:

1. An edition of Beethoven's piano sonata, op.109, was issued in 1821 with the imprint, "Berlin in der Schlesingerschen Buch- und Musikhandlung." There is a second issue, printed from the same plates, but with a new title page, on which the imprint now reads, "Berlin, bey A.M. Schlesinger; Paris, bey Moritz Schlesinger . . ." Moritz Schlesinger moved to Paris around the middle of 1822.[75]

2.   Agents are similarly named on the later issues of Brahms' Hungarian Dances.[76]

3.   Gratuitous misinformation is seen in the Schlesinger edition of Chopin's *Grand Polonaise* in E flat, op.22 (Paris 1836). Schlesinger announced that Mori and Lavenu would be the English publisher; in fact, Wessel was the publisher.[77]

NOTE: Regarding paste-over imprints, see VII.C.1. below.

For information on addresses and directories from particular countries, see the National Reports below, item B.

NOTE: Views of early music shops, interior and exterior, have been frequently reproduced on musical editions. See, for instance, the four shown in this book — as a frontispiece (Austrian, c.1835), on p. 22 (French, 1782), on p. 124 (English, c.1825), and as a colophon (American, c.1855).

IV. *Copyright & Registration*

A. OBJECTIVES AND MEANS. Various legislation has been enacted in order to control the output of the press and to remunerate the creator. Although most copyright has been concerned with books, music, like other forms such as maps and engraved reproductions of art, has often been included in the coverage, explicitly or implicitly. (Sometimes it has been purposely excluded, as when music publishers sought the broader benefits of common law coverage.)

> NOTE: Because the practices vary greatly from country to country, and because so little has been studied of this complicated legal matter, there is no single exhaustive historical survey of music copyright as it relates to bibliographical study. Among the important general discussions of this topic are the following:
>
> H.M. Schuster, *Das Urheberrecht der Tonkunst* (Munich 1891).
>
> Bureau de l'Union Internationale pour la Protection des Oeuvres Littéraires et Artistiques, *Recueil des conventions et traités concernant la propriété littéraire et artistique* (Berne 1904).
>
> Hansjörg Pohlmann, *Die Frühgeschichte des musikalischen Urheberrechts (ca.1400– 1800)* (Kassel 1962).
>
> James J. Fuld, "Copyright Laws," in *The Book of World-Famous Music,* 2nd ed. (New York 1971), pp. 16–24.
>
> American Society of Composers, Authors, and Publishers, *ASCAP Copyright Symposium* (New York, 1939– ; annual).

1. The date of copyright is usually the same as the date of first publication; very rarely is the year different. It does sometimes happen, however, that a work is deposited on one date, and first offered for sale on another. In such instances, the latter is considered to be the publication date, not only by bibliographers but also by the laws of most countries.

2. In most countries three steps in the copyright process are relevant to bibliographical work: registration, deposit, and announcement.

B. REGISTRATION. Depending on the terms and the interpretations of the law in question, the date of entry in the officially specified legal record books indicates an intention to publish, the fact that the edition has been published, or either.

1. Some laws provide for registration as evidence of an intention to publish. In theory, the date of entry is a *terminus post quem* for the publication date. In fact, however, the work may already have been published. Usually the dates are not more than a few weeks apart, although in some instances the difference may amount to several years. Some titles were registered but never published. Some were eventually published under circumstances quite different from those implied or stated in the original registration. For instance, the title, the publisher, or the opus number may be different.

2. Regardless of the different laws, registration usually took place about the time of publication. The cataloguer should thus accept a date of registration as the probable date of publication.

3. Most national registration records are unpublished. If they are preserved, they are likely to be found in the national library of the country.

C. DEPOSITORY COPIES. Such copies generally give the exact date of deposit, entered by hand on the title page or cover. These copies are usually preserved, if at all, in the national library or in designated depository libraries. In some countries, the laws provided specifically that copies could be deposited at any time and were required only for special purposes (i.e., upon demand, for renewal of a copyright, or as evidence in case of litigation).

1. Some publishers made a practice of saving up copies and sending them in as a group at one time.

> **EXAMPLES:** See O.W. Neighbour & Alan Tyson, *English Music Publishers' Plate Numbers* (London 1965), pp. 11–12, also Tyson, *The Authentic English Editions of Beethoven* (London 1963), pp. 131–45, *passim.*; Troupenas in Paris, according to Philip Gossett, deposited many of his publications several years after they first appeared.

(c.) 2. A copy was occasionally deposited before copies were formally offered for sale to the public. When this fact can be determined, the depository copy should be regarded as a pre-publication copy, similar to sample and review copies, differing in function (if probably not in content) from the earliest copy of the published edition. A few countries, such as the United States, required the deposit of a title page (which may or may not appear on the earliest copy) at the time of registration.

D. DATED STATEMENTS. Very few nations have required a date in the edition itself as part of the copyright statement. In fact, dates occur only in editions for which protection is claimed in nations with terms of copyright extending from the date of registration rather than from the date of the creator's death.

1. Dated copyright statements are not necessarily evidence that the copy in question was published in that year. (Indeed, in a re-issue or a new edition from 1845 of a work first published and copyrighted in 1841, it would be dishonest to say "Copyright 1845," since such a statement suggests that the term of protection was four years longer than it really was.)

> EXAMPLE: The Schuberth first edition of Robert Schumann's *Album für die Jugend,* published in Hamburg in January 1849, bears a United States copyright notice with the date of 1846.[78] (See also Figure 162 for a similar notice.)

2. In countries which required no date in the copyright statement, the form of the statement itself is often typical of a certain time.

> EXAMPLE: The title page of the Lucca edition of Donizetti's *La Favorita* announces that the edition was being published in accordance with the copyright laws of 19 October 1846.[79]

3. The presence of a statement is evidence that the text was subject to proprietary rights. Unless otherwise stated, these rights belonged to the publisher.

a. In fact, publishers used their statements ambiguously and often indiscriminately, sometimes with intent to deceive. The German phrase, "Eigentum des Verlegers" — which is definitely not the same as copyright — was frequently intended to be misunderstood.

b. It occasionally happens that an edition with no notice included on it is cited in the official registration records, and/or a depository copy is located.

c. Among the topics which need to be investigated by music bibliographers is the precise meaning of the term "piracy." Special attention should be given to the question of why the authorized publishers so seldom went to the trouble of announcing their rights.

> EXAMPLES: Copyright statements may be seen in Figures 162, 223, 232, 233.

E. PRIVILEGES. In many ways, royal or official privileges should be viewed as the predecessors of formal copyright. Such privileges, which took various forms in various countries, can generally be categorized as either exclusive or restrictive. The exclusive privileges covered all works of a certain kind, i.e., all printed music (as was the exclusive property of the Ballard family in France up to the time of the Revolution). Exclusive privileges seldom required any of the three typical forms of evidence discussed above (i.e., registration records, depository copies, or specific announcement of the privilege, at least such as would typically bear a publication date). The restrictive privileges, on the other hand, covered specific titles; and the editions of these titles often bear a full transcript of the privilege, which is dated. The date of the privilege is a *terminus post quem* for the publication date of the edition involved.

For futher information on copyright in particular countries, see the National Reports below, item F.

V. *Announcement*

A. ADVERTISEMENT IN CONTEMPORARY JOURNALS. Some publishers made a practice of announcing their new editions in newspapers, literary or musical periodicals, or learned journals, as well as in the special supplementary announcements to some of these ("Intelligenzblätter"). In principle, the date of the announcement should be an accurate indication of the date of publication. (See the National Reports below, item G.)

1. Often, however, editions were saved up for listing as a group. Sometimes the editions announced were delayed in printing (see the Example in V.C.1. below).

2. Announcements in journals were often repeated several times, occasionally even years later. It is essential that the announcement used for dating purposes should be the earliest one. (While the location of the earliest notice may be difficult when an incomplete run of the journal is being consulted, the date of this notice may be found to be stated or encoded in the announcement, especially since standing type was generally used for such notices. Often the crucial information consists of some figure indicating the number of times which the announcement was scheduled to appear.)

B. ADVERTISEMENT IN OTHER EDITIONS.

1. Another publication, or different works by the same composer, may be mentioned on the title page (or, rarely, in the music) of one edition. Typically, the imprint is followed by the statement, "Where may be had the following recent publications" (see Figures 6–11). Closely related are the "series passe-partout title pages" (VI.D.3.a.iii. below), and other cumulative title listings (VI.D.5.below).

NOTE: In Figure 44, on the windows of the Mayhew music shop, may be seen a catalogue of sorts, i.e., the titles of various editions which could be purchased inside.

2. A supplementary "plate catalogue" may be included, printed either (a.) from separate plates, so as to be an integral part of the copy itself (see I.D.6.b. above), or (b.) on the wrappers (see VI.D.5. below).

> NOTE: Catalogues of type (a.) are coming to be known as "Johansson catalogues," from the studies of the French and Dutch lists.

3. Such advertisements are useful in the dating of both the edition cited and the edition in which the citation appears. The date of one, when known, is a *terminus* for the other.

4. The different plate catalogues in different copies of the same edition prove useful in determining variant states.

> EXAMPLE: The extant copies of the de la Chevardière edition of Monsigny's *Le cadi dupé* (first performed 4 February 1761) have several different catalogues. For instance, one Library of Congress copy has a 1762 catalogue (Johansson, p. 65); a second Library of Congress copy has a 1763 catalogue (Johannson, p. 67); while a Stockholm copy has the 1765 catalogue (Johansson, facs. 50). Presumably there are other copies with still different catalogues, probably one with a 1761 catalogue.[80]

C. SEPARATE PUBLISHER'S AND DISTRIBUTOR'S CATALOGUES.

These offer a *terminus ante quem* for the publication date of all editions which they list.

> NOTE: Such catalogues have never been described bibliographically. Publisher's catalogues will be the subject of the next major project of the Commission for Bibliographical Research. Distributor's catalogues, on the other hand, are of two kinds: catalogues issued by retail merchants, who almost always were dealers in musical instruments, equipment, and supplies, rather than in printed books; and catalogues of music loan and rental libraries, which consisted of manuscripts as well as printed materials for use in performance.
>
> Among the most important catalogues are those issued in Leipzig by the firm of Breitkopf between 1762 and 1787. The importance and fascination of this set is amply evident from the numerous references in the scholarly literature, especially since the appearance of the facsmilie reprint edited by Barry S. Brook (New York 1966). The matter of the exact dates for some of the supplements (see the point immediately below) remains open to question, however, and therefore the precise meaning of the dating information remains to be determined.[81]

1. The accuracy of the catalogue date needs to be probed in matters of close dating. For a thorough discussion of this matter, see Cari Johansson, *J.J. & B. Hummel* (Stockholm 1972), 1, 15–16.

(C.1) **EXAMPLE:** C.F. Abel's symphonies, op.10, were advertised in the *London Chronicle* on 15 May 1773. The same edition, however, is listed in Supplement VII of the Breitkopf catalogue, dated 1772.[82] While it is possible that the announcement in the newspaper was either belated or a repetition of an earlier announcement, it is just as likely that the Breitkopf catalogue was misdated.

2. Sometimes the groupings of titles toward the end of a list in a catalogue will suggest which of the works may have been issued just before the catalogue appeared.

3. Often the absence of a price is evidence that the edition in question is still in preparation.

4. The importance of a particular catalogue is determined by its relationship to other catalogues of the same publisher, which may be cumulated in it, which may supplement it, or in which it may later be cumulated.

D. NATIONAL BIBLIOGRAPHIES. In the period 1700–1860 there existed few current national bibliographies; and music was usually considered to be outside their purview.

E. FUTURE PUBLICATION. Often a citation mentions publications "soon to appear." (In principle, the word "soon" must always be discounted.) In such instances, the date of the source (usually a journal or another edition: see V.A. or V.B.1. above) becomes a *terminus post quem* for the publication date of the edition cited; while the publication date of the edition cited becomes a *terminus ante quem* for the copy in which the reference appears.

For further information on such catalogues, see the various National Reports below, item E.

VI. *House Practices*

A. BIBLIOGRAPHIC EVIDENCE. In many ways, some obvious and some subtle, a publisher and his workmen prepared their editions in order to serve and to attract purchasers. The materials they used (plates, incising tools, paper, and ink) and the practices they employed (in notation, lay-out, design, and decoration) were also typical of their time. Such matters may or may not also be individually characteristic of earlier or later times.

> **NOTE:** Philip Gaskell, *A New Introduction to Bibliography* (Oxford 1972) is recommended as a survey of the field, with emphasis on type-set printed books.

1. Occasionally we are fortunate to have documentary evidence re-garding printing "house practices." When this happens, we are in a position to establish terminal dates.

> **EXAMPLES:** From archival sources we know that Breitkopf began printing from type in 1756 and that Vollweiler introduced music lithography in England around 1806.

2. Usually, however, we are forced to work from the evidence of the editions which we examine. While bibliographical evidence is readily apparent and hard to question, its use in dating is mostly based on inductive logic, which can lead to nothing more definite than probable dates. "We know of no French music lithographs preceding those of Mme. Verney in 1802" is not the same statement as, "There were no French music lithographs before 1802." The likelihood that inferred dates are accurate increases as the total number of related editions examined reaches 100 per cent. of the total; but there still exists the possibility of an exception to the rule — perhaps the very edition in consideration.

(A.) 3. Most of the findings of music bibliography have been made by scholars studying particular musical texts — "editors," as discussed in I.C.2. above — as well as by other scholars serving the research needs of editors. Only within the past two generations have bibliographers entered the picture, using the findings of editors for their own purposes and discovering facts of their own which have in turn been useful to editors. The work of the bibliographer is essentially different from that of the editor in that it attempts to study a unity of production rather than a unity of text (e.g., the editions produced by Artaria, rather than the editions of Beethoven's *Fidelio*). A model for the work of the bibliographer may be constructed along the following systematic lines:

a. Identification of a unit of study (i.e., the output of one country, city, or firm) from a specific historically defined period; and/or in a bibliographically defined genre.

b. Location of as many copies as possible of the editions produced within the unit of study.

c. Examination of the copies, in search of distinctive variables.

d. Dating the variables by establishing the dates of particular copies which contain or do not contain the variables.

i. In planning a study along such lines, the investigator should understand at the outset that there is no assurance that such variables exist, that he will find them, that they can be dated, or that the dates will not contradict other evidence which he has found.

ii. The dates in question may be of several kinds:

a'. Terminal dates ("My publisher used a particular punch beginning in 1828.")

b'. Approximate dates ("My publisher used upright format in his editions around 1828.")

c'. Negative approximate dates ("My publisher did not use oblong format in his editions around 1828.") which are not quite comparable to b'. above.

iii. Speculative dating of the undated copies can be based on the variables contained in dated copies.

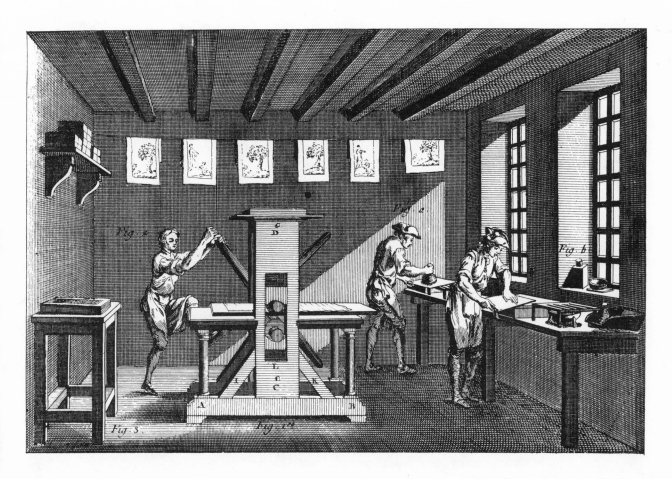

Figure 20. **A FRENCH ENGRAVER'S SHOP IN 1751.** Notice the sheets drying as well as the pressman using his foot.

4. It should be remembered that most matters of execution are the work of engravers, who may have worked for several publishers. Often one large publisher handled the printing for smaller ones (see Figures 186–7).

B. PAPER AND WATERMARKS. The design of watermarks in paper, as well as the distinctive texture and placement of the chain and wire lines in the paper, often suggest a date of the manufacture of the paper, good usually within a span of five or at most ten years. But the date of the paper manufacture bears no consistent fixed relationship to the date of a particular copy of a published edition. Furthermore, the practice of imitating the designs of the well-known papermakers was apparently rather widespread.

> NOTE: According to Professor LaRue, "for the period c.1675–c.1825 we may date a musical manuscript within approximately five years on either side of a date established for its water mark by collateral evidence."[83] In the absence of evidence to the contrary, we may safely say the same of printed music, remembering of course that the date applies to the impression of copies and not necessarily to the edition, issue, or state (see I.D.4.a.i. above, especially the example cited). Obviously the paper was made before the copy in question was printed on it; and thus the manufacture of the paper is a terminus post quem for the impression of any copies concerned. But the impression may be a very late one, and the edition itself (or the issue, or state) may in fact have appeared some time before the batch of paper was manufactured.

1. Watermarks in paper moulds tend to deteriorate, as the wires of the mould "migrate" in the course of becoming detached from the mould. Filigranists can often tell which of two sheets coming from the same pair of moulds was manufactured earlier.

2. Since watermarks tend to have national characteristics, the general area of manufacture can often be suggested even when the specific paper mill can not.

3. Several nations, notably Great Britain, have at times legally required the inclusion of the date in the design of the watermark: or the entire watermark may consist of a date.

4. In general, the work of recent scholars suggests that watermarks are mostly useful in establishing the general region where and the approxi-

mate date when manuscript copies were produced. At the same time, their importance in the study of printed music will increase as bibliographers, having solved their important problems of dating, may turn their attention to the study of different impressions of the same work.

IMPORTANT WRITINGS ON WATERMARKS

General Bibliographies

E.J. Labarre, *A Short Guide to Books on Watermarks* (Hilversum 1955). Translated as "Bücher über Wasserzeichen; Eine Bibliographie," *Philobiblon,* 1 (1957), 237–49.

General Writings

Theo Gerardy, *Datieren mit Hilfe von Wasserzeichen* (Bücheburg 1964).

Ove K. Nordstrand, "Beta-Radiographie von Wasserzeichen," *Papiergeschichte,* 17 (1967), 25–8.

J.S.G. Simmons, "The Leningrad Method of Watermark Reproduction," *The Book Collector,* 10 (1961), 329–30.

Allan H. Stevenson, "New Uses of Watermarks as Bibliographical Evidence," *Studies in Bibliography,* 1 (1948–9), 149–82.

——, "Watermarks are Twins," *Studies in Bibliography,* 4 (1951–2), 57–91.

——, "Beta-Radiography and Paper Research," *VII International Congress on Paper Historians, Communications* (Oxford 1967), 159–68.

Karl Theodor Weiss, *Handbuch der Wasserzeichenkunde* (Leipzig 1962).

Watermarks in Musical Documents

Frederick Hudson, "Concerning the Watermarks in the Manuscripts and Early Prints of G.F. Handel," *Music Review,* 20 (1059), 7–27.

——, "Wasserzeichen in Händelschen Manuskripten und Drucken," in *Konferenzbericht: Händel-Ehrung der Deutschen Demokratischen Republik* (Leipzig 1961), 193–206.

——, *Kritischer Bericht* for G.F. Händel, *Sechs Concerti Grossi, Opus 3* (Hallische Händel-Ausgabe, IV/11; Kassel, Leipzig 1963), especially pp. 34–49, 119–22.

Jan LaRue, "Die Datierung von Wasserzeichen im 18. Jahrhundert," *Bericht über den Internationalen Musikwissenschaftlichen Kongress, Wien, Mozartjahr 1956* (Graz, Köln 1958), pp. 318–23.

——, "Abbreviated Description for Watermarks," *Fontes artis musicae,* 4 (1957), 26–8.

——, "Some National Characteristics of 18th-Century Watermarks," *Journal of the American Musicological Society,* 9 (1956), 237.

——, "Watermarks and Musicology," *Acta musicologica,* 33 (1961), 120–46.

——, "Classification of Watermarks for Musicological Purposes," *Fontes artis musicae,* 13 (1966), 59–63.

18th-CENTURY WATERMARKS. *Figure 21 (above)*: French ("T. Dupuy fin")' used in a Huberty edition which bears a privilege dated 1757.

Figure 22 (above): English, used c.1780. "Pro patria" paper, which was also manufactured in Holland, was typically of high quality. *Figure 23 (left)*: Swiss, used c.1765.

MORE 18th-CENTURY WATERMARKS.
Figure 24 (above): Italian, used c.1797.
Figure 25 (left): Spanish, used in a music book dated 1778. *Figure 26 (below):* Bavarian, used in a 1718 manuscript.

—, "Symbols for Analysis: Some Revisions and Extensions," *Journal of the American Musicological Society,* 19 (1966), 403–8.

—, "Wasserzeichen," *Die Musik in Geschichte und Gegenwart,* 14 (Kassel 1968), cols. 265–7.

For further information on watermarks and paper, see the National Reports below, item J. The Rudén study (see XII: Sweden) is particularly important.

(B.)5. Distinctive paper was used by several publishers. Green tinted paper was characteristic of Böhme in Hamburg around 1800, and of Breitkopf in Leipzig about this same time. Tinted paper in various colors was also used in France around the time of the Revolution, also in the United States around 1830.

6. Special formats were often used in particular periods and places for particular kinds of music.

   a. By 1850, four main sizes had come to predominate:[84]

> Folio format (34 × 27 cm.)
> Edition format (31 × 24 cm.)
> Parisian format (26 × 18 cm.)
> Study score (19 × 14 cm.)

NOTE: The evolution of the word "format," from the bibliographer's narrow sense involving folding of paper (quarto, octavo, duodecimo) to the current sense, which is roughly synonymous with layout and determined mostly by the size of the page, is reflected in the usage above.

Edition format began to appear more frequently around 1870 for the popular, less expensive "Edition" series of standard works, as issued by Litolff, Peters, and Breitkopf & Härtel (i.e., B. & H. Volksausgabe). It was at first known as "Litolff Format," for the earliest (1864) of the "Edition" series (see II.B.3.b. above).

   b. Oblong format was widely used in musical editions. Oblong folio opera vocal scores were issued in Italy before c.1850; hence the term "Italian format" is applied to them, in contradistinction to "Parisian format" (above). In general, the following comprise the main uses of oblong format (folio unless otherwise indicated) between 1700 and 1860:

> In Great Britain, opera vocal scores, 1740–1800
> In France, song collections, 1720–1750 (edition format)

In France, parts for small instrumental ensembles, 1750–1790
In Austria and Germany, various editions, 1780–1810
In Germany, various editions in small sizes, 1700–1760
In Italy, almost everything before 1850

NOTE: Upright formats were also often used for the kinds of editions mentioned above. "Two violin sonatas had been planned to appear as [Beethoven's] op.23. But the violin part of the first sonata was engraved in upright format, that of the second in oblong format; and shortly after publication it was decided to avoid this incongruity by reissuing the sonatas separately, as op.23 and op.24."[85]

For a discussion of the origins of even smaller formats, see Cecil Hopkinson, "The Earliest Miniature Scores," *Music Review,* 33 (1972), 138–44.

For a discussion of music formats before 1700, see the Compiler's "Oblong Format in Early Music Books," *The Library,* 5th series, 26 (1971), 312–24.

For an example of an engraver's confusion over matters of imposition, see the Walsh edition (1730) of *A Choice Collection of Aires and Duets for two German Flutes.*[86] In each four-page gathering, the second through fourth pages are reversed in numbering (i.e., 1, 4, 3, 2, 5, 8, 7, 6, 9, 12, 11, 10, &c.). While the numbering is mostly wrong, the contents appear in the correct order. (The assembly of this edition is a particularly complicated one, with the music printed on one side of the page only, and the duets arranged so that the two parts appear on facing pages.)

C. TECHNOLOGY OF REPRODUCING MUSIC.
During the period covered in this study, three major innovations occurred which greatly affected music publishing. (Several related technological matters should also be treated as part of this discussion.)

1. The use of punches on soft pewter plates, instead of hand-drawn or etched lines on hard copper plates, is thought to have been introduced by Walsh in London around 1695 (see VI.E.3. below).

NOTE: The exact metallic constitution of the plates has not been studied. The cracking of Viennese plates mentioned above (I.D.4.a.ii.) was probably due to the particular alloy involved. A study of the plates cannot be made, however, until the plates have been located, or until some records of the suppliers have turned up — which events seem unlikely. (Plates of the Augsburg firm of Gombart are known to exist at the Stadtarchiv in Augsburg, while a few London plates from c.1820 are in the possession of Alan Tyson. The existence of still others, as discovered, should be publicized, or called to the attention of the Compiler or other scholars involved in the present study.)

(C.) 2. The process of lithography was developed by Alois Senefelder between 1793 and 1800. See Senefelder's treatise (London 1819); F.M. Ferchl, *Übersicht der Inkunabelsammlung der Lithographie* (Munich 1856); and Michael Twyman, *Lithography* (London 1970). The role of music in the early history of lithography is a very important one which only now is beginning to be studied.

> Examples of early lithography are seen in Figures 131, 134, 145–7, 201, and 213.

3. Use in music publishing of the various transfer and offset lithography processes, according to Deutsch, dates from "about 1866."[87] But almost certainly there are earlier music covers than this (probably from France as in the so-called "Jullien albums"), and most likely some musical text itself, printed by such methods. The lithographic transfer (designated by Deutsch with the term *Umdruck;* Brahms called it *Überdruck*) can most easily be distinguished from other lithographs by the exact identity of the shapes of all instances of a particular sign, such as would result from their having been executed by the same punch.

> NOTE: There are instances of copies having been printed from engraved plates by two different methods. Of Peter Heise's *Digte fra Middelalderen,* for example, on 1 June 1875, there were printed "500 Overtryk" (that is, 500 copies by lithographic transfer), "100 Pladetryk" (that is, 100 copies directly from the plates), and "5 fine" (that is, five presentation copies on large, heavy paper).[88]

4. The nature of the presses used to print music, and the changes in these presses between 1700 and 1850 have not been studied. Presumably engraved music was printed on a typical "rolling press" (see Figures 20, 27–8, 30), no different from the presses used for such other engravings as maps, portraits, currency, and the like. But this matter has never been investigated, and no original source material relating to it has been cited in the standard writings. At the same time, the eye, and even the fingers, can be trained to recognize which of the three processes were employed to print a particular sheet. Movable type, for instance, tends to dig into the sheet, although the finer the presswork, the less will be the impressions. An engraved plate leaves an embossed "margin" around the edge of the page (as seen conspicuously in Figures 4, 48, 99, and elsewhere). Frequently very fine streaks appear on the page in the area touched by the plate (although more typically in 16th and 17th-century copperplate engravings than in later music work). The

Figure 27. **A LATE 17th-CENTURY ENGLISH ENGRAVER'S SHOP.**

(C.) texture of the paper in this same area also appears flattened — indeed "ironed" — in contrast to the area beyond the margin, which is more pristine. In addition, the ink is thick, producing a shininess which can be seen and a ridge which can be felt. In contrast, the lithographic printing effect is quite flat.

5. The rise of stereotyping, and its application to music, needs to be investigated. While music is not specifically cited among the early efforts of the press, at least one kind of attempt at a kind of stereotyping was undertaken by Edward Cowper in 1827. Early stereotype music was generally in the tradition of type-set books more than engraved music; and thus it will usually bear a date on their title pages, which may or may not be the meaningful one for bibliographical purposes.

> Among the writings which treat 19th-century printing technology, the four below (ranging from the general survey to the compilation of little-studied source material) are important:
>
> W. Turner Berry and H. Edmund Poole, *Annals of Printing* (London 1966). See especially 217—18.
>
> Michael Twyman, *Printing, 1770—1970: An Illustrated History* (London 1970).
>
> Elizabeth M. Harris, "Experimental Graphic Processes in England, 1800—1859," *Journal of the Printing Historical Society,* 4 (1968) 33—86; 5 (1969), 41—80; 6 (1970), 53—89.
>
> *Printing Patents: Abridgements of Patent Specifications Relating to Printing, 1617—1857* (London 1859; supplement, 1878; reprinted together, London 1969; Printing Historical Society Publications, 6.).

6. No studies have been located which analyze the inks used in early music. The following important innovations occurred during the period studied in this book:[89]

1763:	Logwood inks probably first introduced.
1770:	Indigo first used in inks (Eisler).
1780:	Steel pens invented. (NB: This invention may have taken place soon after 1700.)
c.1803:	Metal pens first placed on the market.
c.1816:	Colored inks using pigments first manufactured in England.
1820:	The invention of the modern type of metal nib.
1836:	Introduction of iron-gall inks containing indigo (Stephens).
1856:	Discovery of the first coal-tar dyestuff (Perkin's mauve), leading to the use of such dyestuffs in colored inks.

Figure 28. A LATE 18th-CENTURY ENGLISH ENGRAVER'S SHOP, SHOWN IN CARICATURE BY THOMAS ROWLANDSON.

Important studies include the following:

David N. Carvalho, *Forty Centuries of Ink* (New York 1904).

William B. Gamble, "Chemistry and Manufacture of Writing and Printing Inks: A List of References ... ," *Bulletin of the New York Public Library*, 29 (1925), 579–91, 625–77, 706–41.

C.H. Bloy, *A History of Printing Ink, Balls, and Rollers, 1440–1850* (London 1967).

D. THE EVIDENCE OF THE TITLE. Besides serving to identify the work, a title statement may be useful for dating in several possible ways.

1. The evolution of the text of the title statement has not, for the most part, been systematically studied, although specialists have usually relied on such information in a highly "impressionistic" way for purposes of assigning approximate dates (i.e., within a decade or two). Among the important kinds of evidence in the title statement are the following:

a. The prominence given to the name of the composer, and the specific titles and adjectives used to refer to him (i.e., "celebrated," "late," "Master of Music to ... ").

b. The title itself (see VII.B.5. below), an opus number (see VII.A.2. below), the dedication (see VII.B. below), the price (see VII.F. below), the imprint (see III.C.,D. above), and the copyright statement (see IV.D. above).

c. The placement in a numbered series. As with opus numbers we should presume, in the absence of evidence to the contrary, that number 5 appeared after number 4 and before number 6.

NOTE: See II. above, especially II.B.2. regarding the complications involved in distinguishing such series from plate-number series. In general, many of the principles used in dating from plate numbers can also apply to dating from numbered series.

d. The language of the title page. In the years around 1700, for instance, Italian tended to be used rather than the vernacular language, while around 1800 there was a tendency to use French. In Germany, however, Italian forms tended to be popular around 1800, until the re-emergence of German forms about 1815. The spelling "Klavier" was preferred in Germany around 1780 while the spelling "Clavier" was preferred around 1800, for instance.[90]

THE THREE PRESSES IN AMERICA IN 1836. *Figure 29 (top)*: A letter press for movable type, specifically one of the new 19th-century iron hand presses. *Figure 30 (lower left)*: A rolling press for engraving. *Figure 31 (lower right)*: A press for lithography.

(D.) 2. The design and the decoration of music title pages have been the subject of considerable interest. Among the important studies and anthologies of music title pages are the following:

John Grand-Carteret, *Les titres illustrés et l'image au service de la musique* (Turin 1904).

W.E. Imeson, *Illustrated Music-Titles and Their Delineators* (London 1912).

Walter von zur Westen, *Musiktitel aus vier Jahrhunderten; Festschrift anlässlich der 75-jährigen Bestehens der Firma C.G. Röder* (Leipzig 1921).

Marian Hannah Winter, *Art Scores for Music* (Brooklyn, N.Y. 1939).

Gottfried S. Fraenkel, *Pictorial and Decorative Title Pages from Music Sources* (New York 1968).

Richard Schaal, *Musiktitel aus fünf Jahrhunderten* (Wilhelmshaven 1972), which includes a useful bibliography, pp. 23—7.

Otto Erich Deutsch, "Schwinds Rossini-Vignetten und verwandte Arbeiten aus seiner Wiener Jugendzeit," *Mitteilungen der Gesellschaft für Vervielfältigende Kunst* (Wien), 49 (1926), 37—47, among the best studies of a particular group of illustrated covers.

NOTE: Deutsch has discussed some of the problems of transcribing music title pages,[91] and identified eleven typical problem areas. "Notwithstanding generally accepted bibliographical practice and the advantages of employing it wherever possible, it appears to me a sheer impossibility to describe successfully engraved (or lithographed) musical title-pages by the orthodox method used by bibliographers." Further, "In matters unessential it [i.e., the transcription of title pages by conventional methods] says too much, while of the essentials it says too little."[92]

3. "Passe-partout" title pages were printed from one plate which was intended to be used again in other editions. Such plates were usually artistically executed, probably on copper rather than pewter. They contained, besides extensive decoration, such information as would remain appropriate to a number of different editions, e.g., the imprint. The remaining information was added to the particular edition.

a. There are several kinds of passe-partout titles.

i. The additional information was supplied on a second engraved plate, for which an open area was left (see Figures 32—6).

ii. The additional information was intended to be filled in by hand. It might consist of the full identification of the composer and the title, or only of an opus or series number.

iii. In the 19th century particularly, publishers often used a

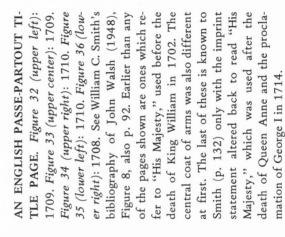

AN ENGLISH PASSE-PARTOUT TITLE PAGE. *Figure 32 (upper left): 1709. Figure 33 (upper center): 1709. Figure 34 (upper right): 1710. Figure 35 (lower left): 1710. Figure 36 (lower right):* 1708. See William C. Smith's bibliography of John Walsh (1948), Figure 8, also p. 92. Earlier than any of the pages shown are ones which refer to "His Majesty," used before the death of King William in 1702. The central coat of arms was also different at first. The last of these is known to Smith (p. 132) only with the imprint statement altered back to read "His Majesty," which was used after the death of Queen Anne and the proclamation of George I in 1714.

(D.3.a.) "series passe-partout," on which was listed all of the works in a specific publisher's series. The particular work contained in the edition in question was designated by a hand-written mark on the title page.

iv. Imbault in Paris in the 1790s used what Hermann Baron has called a "demi-passe-partout," something of a variant of i. above which consists of one plate for the top half and another for the bottom half of the title page.

v. In Italy in the 1780s and 1790s, a kind of publication in manuscript" was achieved by adding passe-partout title pages, with full imprint information on them, to manuscript copies.

> EXAMPLES: Various passe-partout pages are shown in the anthologies mentioned in VI.D.2. above. See, for instance:
>
> Fraenkel, nos. 148, 176, 177, 180, 198(?)
>
> Schaal, pp. 104(?), 112, 115, 126, 129, 138, 140, 147, 156, 161, 164, 166, 171, 172, 174, 177, 181
>
> Zur Westen, pp. 64, Tafeln 94, 95

b. Since passe-partout plates were used over a period of many years, the date suggested by the title is not necessarily that of the edition.

> EXAMPLES:
>
> 1. The first three issues of the Walsh edition of Handel's *Messiah* use a plate which had been used earlier for *Judas Maccabaeus*.[93]
>
> 2. Grand-Carteret, p. 81, assigns a date of 1793–4 to the passe-partout cover for a Hummel edition of Giornovichi quartets. He does this on the basis of costume styles in the illustration. Johansson, however, has assigned a date of 1798/1802 for this edition, primarily on the basis of the plate number 1109.[94]
>
> 3. Five different imprint statements may be seen in the various states of one Walsh passe-partout title page. The plate, designed by Collins, was used as early as 1699 and as late as 1740.[95]
>
> 4. Late impressions and issues of the first edition of Brahms' *Ein deutsches Requiem* can be distinguished by the absence or presence of a tinted title page.[97]
>
> > NOTE: Minor changes, indicative of new or altered plates, can often be detected in passe-partout titles used around 1850.[96]

4. Caption titles, found mainly on short musical works, reflect the fashions in design and calligraphy. Captions can best be studied in the editions of publishers who specialized in popular music and from countries which are associated with popular music.

    a. Fashions in design and calligraphy between 1700 and 1860 have not been studied extensively. One of the few important studies is Nicolette Gray, *XIXth Century Ornamented Types and Title Pages* (London 1938).

    b. In the course of history, caption titles became more elaborate. In England around 1700, they seldom filled more than 3 cm. at the head of the page (as in Figures 46 and 47); they were often balanced by the imprint at the foot of the page. By 1800 the caption title commonly filled the top third of the title page, and by 1850 the top half. (See various figures in this book; Figures 67—8 are exceptional.) By 1750 the imprint had typically become a part of the caption, usually the bottom element of the caption just above the first system of music. With the rise of the decorative music cover in the 19th century, the caption diminished in importance. Much of its descriptive and promotional information moved to the cover, leaving for it only a simple statement which identified the work and the composer.

    c. Patterns of imitation can be detected in the layouts of caption titles (see Figures 226—9). For further discussion, see VI.F. below.

    d. Occasionally one sees copies of an edition with the entire caption area left blank. Such copies are states, we should presume, which predate later states containing the caption. From such copies we may also deduce that two workmen contributed to the engraving, one of whom did the music, the other the caption.

5. Often included on title pages were cumulative lists, which consisted either of series passe-partout title pages (VI.D.3.a.iii. above), or included listings of other editions which were available from the publisher (III.C. above). Often two extant copies of the same edition will have two different listings, one with more titles than the other. While the copy with more titles presumably appeared later than the one with fewer titles, a careful inspection of the copy with fewer titles will occasionally reveal the titles had been deleted from it, in which case it would be the later one.

NOTE: The question arises as to whether such changes are evidence of a new issue or a new state. Was there in fact any change in the circumstances of publication, such as would imply re-issue? One could argue that there was — that the "total package," of which the copy in question was one part, was now different. Furthermore, the copy can often be assigned a very specific date on the basis of the particular titles which appear on the list — provided that one can be reasonably sure that the titles had actually appeared, and were not merely being announced (see III.C.2.,3.). (A new issue, it will be remembered, can characteristically be dated, while a new state usually cannot be.) One could also argue, however, that the circumstances of publication were really not different because of the enlargement or condensation of the list; and that the date of the issue is the appropriate one. The advertisement should be disregarded in the presence of more fundamental evidence. (Indeed, we really have here two separate arguments going on at once, one over terminology and the other over dating.) An example, celebrated in the United States, is Carrie Jacobs Bond's *Seven Songs,* published by the composer in 1901, with a catalogue on the back cover which changed over later years.

6. Wrappers are often found on certain kinds of musical editions. Breitkopf & Härtel, for instance, often used heavy, deeply colored wrappers for their oblong folio editions around 1800; while French publishers frequently used thin, pastel wrappers after 1835. Such covers were usually printed from movable type, at least before 1860, even when the music itself was engraved or lithographed. Unfortunately, these wrappers usually came to be detached in the course of heavy use, or were removed by binders. Occasionally a copy with wrappers will have a title page which names one publisher, and wrappers which name another. These can usually be treated in the same way as copies with "paste-over" imprints (see VII.E.3.c. below).

E. THE MUSICAL NOTATION. The general musical style and medium, the presence of particular distinctive stylistic devices, the instruments specified, and the editorial practices, all contribute to the appearance of the page of music.[98] (See VII.A.3. below, for instance.) The following are among the graphic characteristics which can be useful in dating:

1. The general layout and arrangement of the musical text are important, both in overall conception and in specific details. The work of different engravers simply "looks" different, although the specific factors which cause this are usually very difficult to identify and to de-

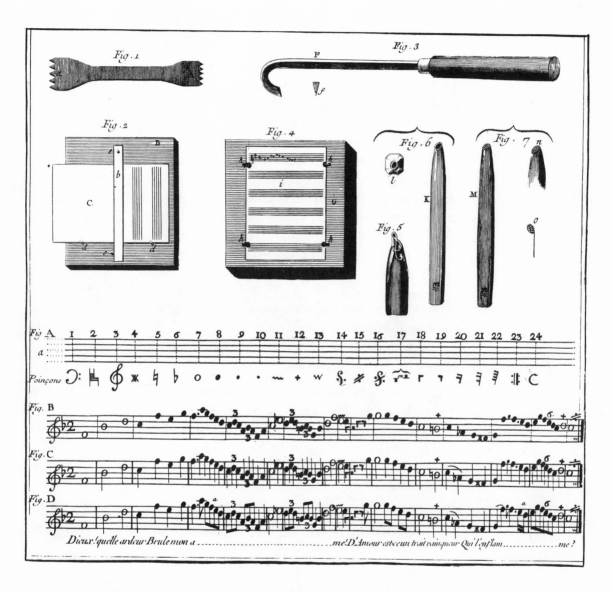

Figure 37. TOOLS OF THE FRENCH MUSIC ENGRAVER IN 1751, AND THE SEQUENCE OF STEPS IN THE ENGRAVING OF A PLATE.

(E.) scribe. Among these factors may be the following:

a. The amount of unused space on the page, and the ways in which the engraver chose to minimize it.

b. The placement of page numbers, plate numbers, and captions.

2. The orthography and style of literary texts also provide valuable clues. Gothic faces were rarely seen, even in German editions, except around 1815. Italic, however, was used extensively, probably because it was so well suited to engraving. The medial "s" disappeared after 1790, in music much as in literature. The French Baroque *financière* was used occasionally in various countries throughout the period 1700–1860 (as in Figure 161), perhaps because it was known to musicians on manuscript captions and storage labels.

3. Punches were used by engravers beginning with the period covered by this study. Their widespread acceptance dates in England from c.1695, in France from c.1740, in Germany from c.1775; or so we say only in a preliminary way, not yet having studied thoroughly such matters. Furthermore, different "series" of punches were probably introduced in different countries at different times. Among the "series" of punches are the following:

a. Note heads, achieved by a simple flattened point, might appear to have been the first punches. Yet it is hard to see that any of these was ever used except in conjunction with more complicated signs. The hand-drawn black note head, in any event, can sometimes be identified through cross-hatching marks, especially in 17th-century engravings.

EXAMPLES: For free-hand engraving, without punches, see Figures 45, 52, 82, and 144.

b. Musical signs, such as the clefs (G, C, and F), sharps and flats, C for the time signature (upright, inverted, or reversed), and rests are next in importance. The G clef seems to be the most distinctive punch of all (see Figures 38–43). Punches appear to be especially useful in assigning editions to their engraver, although there are examples (particularly in Parisian classical editions) of punches being distinctive to the publisher; the same engraver used one set of punches for one publisher, another set for another publisher.

c. Braces enclosing a musical system are often surprisingly characteristic. Those used in 18th-century France, for instance, are distinctively square (see Figures 91–100).

d. Other musical signs that were frequently punched included numbers (for pages, as well as 2, 3, 4, 6, 8 for time signatures); "tr" and other ornaments; "p," "f," "m," "cresc.," and "dim.," for dynamics; and a dotted half-circle fermata (see Figures 60–1 for punches for "Pia." and "For.").

PUNCH FORMS USED IN EARLY BRITISH MUSIC. *Figure 38:* London 1759. *Figure 39:* York: Thomas Harby, 1764. *Figure 40:* London c.1765. *Figure 41:* London c.1770. *Figure 42:* London: Longman & Broderip, 1792. *Figure 43:* Edinburgh: Muir & Wood, c.1815.

e. Fonts of punches for the alphabet were actually introduced some years after the punches for musical signs. (Handwritten texts with punched music may be seen in Figures 46–7, 50, and 90–9.)

f. Slurs are generally drawn with great skill, considering how difficult they are to execute (see, however, Figure 183).

g. The five-pronged "Raster," used for drawing the staff lines in one stroke, was developed at a fairly early time in most countries, although some engravers are said to have preferred individually-drawn staff lines, even until recently. Occasional unevenness of the five lines betrays the fact that the lines were drawn one at a time (as in Figures 55, 62, 82, 191, 218 – bottom line center –, and 222), while parallel

97

E.3.) variations in all five lines (as in the bottom line of Figure 98) betray the use of a Raster. The beginnings and endings of the lines, at the left and right margins, are not as helpful as one might suspect, except in extremely obvious instances. There seem to be no distinguishing heights to the staff in different countries at different times. Small-size staff lines, for use on the same page as large staves (as in piano chamber music; see Figure 177) appear not to have been used extensively before c.1825, perhaps later.

h. Bordered pages (as in Figures 46, 52, and 190) are exceptions, found characteristically only in London around 1700 and in Paris (Edition-format chanson albums) around 1840.

j. Both the style of the handwriting of many engravers and the notational practices they preferred are often distinctive in such matters as the thickness of the slurs, the shape of the flags, the thickness of stems and measure markings. For an understanding of the complicated decisions necessary in arranging musical notation for the best possible legibility, books on musical copying should be consulted, for which Hal Ross, *The Art of Music Engraving and Processing* (Miami 1970), is highly recommended.

k. For dating purposes, the identification of engravers does not seem promising as an area for future study, since the careers of the engravers can almost never be documented. On the other hand, the identification of the distinctive styles of music engraving, as a medium for communicating the composer's intention to the performer, has many interesting implications which need to be uncovered. (In the history of music, there must have been moments when the publisher told the composer, "We can't do what you want," and the composer responded, "You find a way to do it or I'll find another publisher." Conversely, one can imagine the publisher telling the composer, "Our engraver has an idea for a new kind of punch, – or a new arrangement of the text – which would better convey some of the things you want to do in your music.") An interesting thesis could be written, for instance, on the history of the page turn.

4. While the placement and the typography of the page number are distinctive evidence, the pagination itself also becomes of great interest to bibliographers when two or more sets of numbers appear.

a. Multiple pagination is found under several circumstances (see I.D.7.d.). Among them are: (i) separately issued song sheets collected into an anthology (an arrangement found most often in early 18th-century England); (ii) selections from an opera or other sectional work issued as separate numbers; (iii.) selections from one or more collections assembled to make up a new collection; and (iv.) Complete or collected editions made from previously issued separate editions.

b. The several series of page numbers usually appear in contrasting positions on the page, and in contrasting type faces or sizes. These numbers suggest relative dates for the two editions involved.

i. When two sets of numbers appear, the numbers appropriate to the present edition are likely to have been added last, although not necessarily (see Example 1 below).

ii. When an edition appears in two states, one with only the appropriate page numbers and the other with these numbers plus an unused set of numbers, the former is likely to be the earlier of the two states (see Examples 2 and 3 below). But this is not necessarily the case: in the former, the second set of numbers may have been deleted so that traces of the earlier numbers will often be faintly visible (see Example 5 below).

iii. Pages were usually numbered in the outer corners (versos in the upper or lower left, rectos in the upper or lower right); thus any pagination which appears in other positions is likely to have been added after the pagination in the customary positions (see Example 4 below).

EXAMPLES: Multiple pagination is seen in Figure 79. The Smith *Handel: A Descriptive Catalogue* (1970) is a veritable anthology of examples of pagination practices, from which the following are drawn (page numbers from the catalogue are in parentheses):

1. The 1744 editions of *Joseph* (p. 110) have page numbers in the outer top corners. The plates were later used in various of three other publications, for which the page numbers appear in the top center. The plates were then re-assembled in the original order for purposes of printing more copies (i.e., a second state of the edition) of *Joseph*. The latter (p. 111, no. 2) thus contains both of the numbers.

(E.4.) 2. The plates for the 1728 Walsh edition of *Siroe* (p. 69) were used in 1729 for *Apollo's Feast, Book III* (p. 162, no. 5), and then re-assembled for a new printing of *Siroe*. Therefore, there exist two states of *Siroe*: one (p. 69, no. 2) from 1728 *without* the second set of page numbers, and the other (p. 69, no. 3) from 1729 or later *with* the second set. A later version (p. 69, no. 6), from c.1747, has still more page numbers.

3. The plates for *Xerxes* (p. 68) were also used in other collections. In addition to the original numbers, the later state of *Xerxes* contains added page numbers, either in the top center (for *Apollo's Feast, Book V*) or in the bottom center (for one of several other collections).

4. The *Overtures* (p. 280) were issued in groups of six and later collected in larger groups. The plates of the first set of six, from 1726 (p. 280, no. 1), for instance, were used in 1730 in a collection called *XXIV Overtures* (p. 282, no. 9). For the 1730 collection, page numbers were needed in the top center; but the 1726 collection had already been numbered there. Thus, the earlier numbers had to be removed and re-engraved in the bottom center.

5. The plates from c.1726 for *Elisa and Rodelinda* (p. 62, no. 9) have page numbers which were erased for *Apollo's Feast*. These plates were later incorporated into a c.1750 edition containing only *Rodelinda* (p. 63, no. 13). Some plates from this edition were altered for a new edition of *Apollo's Feast* (p. 164, no. 12), and used thus for a new printing of *Rodelinda*, c.1755 (p. 63, no. 14).

More than two sets of page numbers are possible. Deutsch refers to an example of quadruple pagination, but does not cite the copy.[99]

5. Occasionally engravers signed their names or initials on their editions (see Figures 65, 87, 96, and 134, among others). This information has so far proven to be more interesting than useful in dating, partly because our information on early music engravers remains even more elusive than that on music publishers.

a. The music engraver and the person who engraved a decorative title page for an edition were probably not often the same person. The former worked with punches and hand engraving tools on soft metal; the latter often used various engraving processes on hard metal. The former performed the largely routine task of transferring a text to a printed surface, while the latter was expected to create an attractive and original artistic design.

b. The name of a workman signed on a title page, furthermore, may be that either of the designer or of the man who executed his design.

Frequently both men are named, and their respective contributions indicated by Latin abbreviations. Although no list of the widely used terms of the 18th and 19th centuries has been located, the terms in Arthur M. Hind, *A Short History of Engraving and Etching* (2nd ed., London 1911), p. 16, while concerned with earlier practice, would appear to be generally applicable.

Composuit	Design conceived by
Delin[eavit]	Draftsmanship by
Exc[udit], or Formis	Literally "printed by," but in earlier practice usually the name of the publisher or the seller
Fecit	Engraved by
Figuravit	Drawn by, i.e., usually the engraver, imitating a composition by another artist
Incidit	Engraved by
Inven[it]	Design conceived by
Pinx[it]	Painted by
Sculpsit	Engraved by, or later, etched by
Sumptibus	At the expense of

c. In 18th-century French editions, the title page often includes the words "Gravé par . . . ." Many of the engravers, it should be noted, were women: see Cecil Hopkinson, *A Dictionary of Parisian Music Publishers* (London 1954), p. 128. We should presume that this person probably engraved both the music and the title page, although in a number of instances it is evident that the person was responsible for only one or the other.

F. PATTERNS OF IMITATION. An edition which is carefully and artistically executed does not by that fact alone necessarily either predate or postdate another edition of the same music which is badly executed. Reprints usually copied the layout (i.e., what is today referred to in music publishing circles as the "Stichbild") of the original, with decorative elements and line endings identical (see Figures 10–11, 106, and 226–9, for example). Reprints often contained mistakes not in the original; but there are instances of mistakes having been corrected, and it was not uncommon for later engravers to have spread out cluttered passages (as in Figure 214, top line), often to arrange for more convenient page turns.

VII. *Other Evidence*

A. THE BACKGROUND OF THE MUSICAL WORK. Often the date of composition helps to suggest a date of publication, the former being a *terminus post quem* for the latter. In turn the date of publication may help to suggest a date of composition.

1. Some composers dated their compositions on the manuscript (e.g., Schubert), while others maintained an index (e.g., Mozart's *Verzeichnüss aller meiner Werke*). The date written on a particular manuscript may in fact be other than the date when the composition was finished, i.e., it may be the date of the completion of copying. This topic is complicated, needing further study most of all by scholars who specialize in the documents of the particular composer.

2. Although the history of opus numbers remains to be written, at this moment it seems safe to generalize by saying that 18th-century opus numbers were *usually* assigned by the publisher, while those of the 19th century were usually assigned by the composer. A 19th-century opus number most likely identifies a work composed later than the work with the number just preceding, and earlier than the work with the number just following. But the peculiarities of opus number chronology are legion. Opus numbers are scarcely dependable or even useful in dating except insofar as they may support or contradict other kinds of evidence. (See, for instance, Example 1 under II.C.2.c. above.)

3. The musical style of a composition can offer the basis for a general impression of a date (but usually, unfortunately, no more specific than within the range of a decade or two). Because of scholarly interest in originality and innovation, we also tend to feel on firmer ground with

the *terminus post quem* than with the *terminus ante quem* ("this is the first appearance of characteristic A" rather than "this is the last appearance of characteristic B"). In matters of musical style, simple and specific matters, such as terminology and notation, may prove to be of greater help in dating than we now realize, as suggested in the following instances:

EXAMPLES:

1. The Beethoven piano sonata, op.7, was issued by Schott, first in 1797 with the title *Grande sonate pour le clavecin ou piano-forte,* and again in 1830 with the title *Grande Sonate pour le piano-forte seul.*[100]

2. Operas issued by Lucca in Milan generally use C clefs in the 1830s and 1840s, and G clefs in later editions. (The former are generally in oblong, Italian format, while the latter are in the less conservative, upright, Parisian format.)[101]

4. The date of a first performance ordinarily is very close to the date of first publication. But there are many exceptions to such a general rule. This kind of evidence should be considered important only in the presence of other supporting evidence.

> **EXAMPLE:** The first performance of Rossini's *Ermione* took place at the Teatro San Carlo, Naples, on 27 March 1819. One duet from this work, was published by the Litografia Priviligiata di Napoli, and bears a date of 30 March 1819.[102]

a. Music intended for a large public audience is likely to have been available very soon after the first performance; while more specialized and imposing works may not have been published until years later, when a demand for copies arose.

b. Association of a published copy with a particular performance (especially of operas) can be determined in several ways. The performers are often named and the content was often altered. Libretti, playbills, and advertisements offer useful bases for comparison.

c. The mention of a specific performer can provide valuable information for dating purposes; but it should also be remembered that performers frequently included favorite works in their repertories for many years.

d. Belated publication often — one might go so far as to say usually — takes place in conjunction with a well publicized revival.

103

B. REFERENCES TO CONTEMPORARY EVENTS AND PERSONS.
These may relate either to the composition or to the publication of the music. They may help in providing either a *terminus* date or an approximate date.

1. The dedication of a work may often be dated through biographical facts about the recipient, i.e., his career, his location, the form of his name, often his exact title. The history of his relationship with the composer is particularly important.

EXAMPLES:

1. Of the early editions of the Clementi sonata, op.41, the first, issued by Artaria in Vienna on 7 January 1804, is dedicated to Franz von Hess. Hess died on 27 January, and the revised London edition, published early in April 1804, was dedicated to the Rev. John Cleaver Banks. There is also a third edition, from Mollo in Vienna, "Consacrées à la memoire de Monsieur de Hess . . . par les Editeurs," and probably issued in the summer of 1804.[103]

2. Some dedications were determined by the publisher, not by the composer, particularly in the 19th century. A later example, from 1839, is the Diabelli edition of Schubert's A-minor piano sonata, op.posth. (Deutsch 784), which was dedicated to Felix Mendelssohn.

3. The complicated relationships between a composer and his patrons result in some unusual predicaments for the scholar. Carl Nielsen's opus 21, for instance, is said to have appeared in two issues, different only in that they were dedicated to two different persons. Beethoven's dedications have been studied by Alan Tyson.[104]

2. Some persons are known today mostly because of their association with a composer or publisher. (One thinks of Schikaneder, described as "preserved in *Zauberflöte* like a gnat in amber.") But often, dates in the careers of these persons are useful in dating.

EXAMPLE: In Walsh editions, references to "Her Majesty" rather than to "His Majesty" (i.e., to Queen Anne, who reigned 1702–1714) are particularly useful. See Figures 32–6.

3. "Occasional music" (*Gelegenheitskompositionen,* i.e., battle pieces, as well as works for dedications, commemorations, coronations, and other specific ceremonies) can be dated from the event to which they refer. It is most important, of course, to determine whether the music was issued *for* the event, or *because of* it; and while this fact is usually self-obvious, it can also be very difficult or even impossible to uncover.

If the music was written for an event, the publication date—presumably very close to the date of the event—is seldom from a different year. On the other hand, if the music was composed because of an event (as with battle pieces), it is important to learn both how quickly the news of the event was circulated and how long the event was likely to have been one of public interest and recollection. (The most celebrated exception to this statement, of course, is the *Chant sur la mort de Joseph Haydn*, composed in 1805 by Cherubini on the false reports of the death of the former composer.)

4.   Song texts often mention persons and events of general public interest. In a very general way, they also reflect the attitudes of their day. Strictly speaking, such evidence is appropriate to dating the composition, not the publication. On the other hand, the two were usually very close, especially for music which was written with a view to widespread public circulation.

5.   Although persons who work extensively with musical titles can frequently associate a general period with a particular title, a proper study of the syntax of such titles has apparently never been made. Besides being of interest in itself, such a study would be useful for purposes of dating editions. While popular song titles are particularly distinctive, the titles of abstract instrumental forms often enjoyed periods of popularity (e.g., "Sinfonia concertante" or "Nocturne"), as did the adjectives used to describe such works (e.g., "celebrated," "new," "brilliant," "delightful," "pathetic"). (See also Example 1 under VII.A.3. above.)

C.   PUBLISHERS' ARCHIVES.   The record books of a publishing firm, along with its printed catalogues and its correspondence with composers and others, are all important sources for the bibliographer. They may also prove to be critical to the editor, and further, when they are made conveniently available in a published transcript, they may be useful to the cataloguer.

NOTE: Of the three sources, the record books are seldom available in published form. However, they have been extensively and effectively used, beginning with Kathi Meyer's study of Schott,[105] and culminating in Alexander Weinmann's *Beiträge* on Viennese publishers. Among the most important compilations of the correspondence between composers and publishers are the following:

Ludwig van Beethoven und seine Verleger, S.A. Steiner und Tobias Haslinger in Wien, Ad. Mart. Schlesinger in Berlin; Ihr Verkehr und Briefwechsel, ed. by Max Unger (Vienna, Berlin 1921).

Beethoven-Briefe an Nicolaus Simrock [and others], ed. by Leopold Schmidt (Berlin 1909).

Johannes Brahms, *Briefe an P.J. Simrock und Fritz Simrock,* ed. by Max Kalbeck. 4 vols. (Brahms, *Briefwechsel,* 9–12; Berlin 1917–1919).

——, *Briefwechsel mit Breitkopf & Härtel, Bartolf Senff, J. Rieter-Biedermann, C.F. Peters, E.W. Fritzsch und Robert Lienau,* ed. by Wilhelm Altmann (Brahms, *Briefwechsel,* 14; Berlin 1920).

Edvard Grieg, *Briefe an die Verleger der Edition Peters, 1866–1907,* ed. by Elsa von Zschinsky-Troxler (Leipzig 1932).

Joseph Haydn und das Verlagshaus Artaria, ed. by Franz Artaria & Hugo Botstiber (Vienna 1909).

Joseph Haydn und Breitkopf & Härtel, ed. by Hermann von Hase (Leipzig 1909).

Felix Mendelssohn, *Briefe an deutsche Verleger,* ed. by Rudolf Elvers (Mendelssohn, *Briefe,* 1; Berlin 1968).

Correspondence between Leopold Mozart and Lotter in Augsburg, also between Mozart's widow and sister with Breitkopf & Härtel and J.A. André, in *Mozart, Briefe und Aufzeichnungen,* ed. by Wilhelm A. Bauer & Otto Erich Deutsch (Kassel 1962–   ), esp. v. 1. pp. 3–48, and v. 4, pp. 206–450.

Richard Wagner, *Briefwechsel mit seinen Verlegern,* ed. by Wilhelm Altmann, 1: *Briefwechsel mit Brietkopf & Härtel* (Leipzig 1911); 2: *Briefwechsel mit B. Schott's Söhne* (Mainz 1911).

Other correspondence of composers is often included in general collections of their correspondence, or in special articles.[106]

D. LISTS OF SUBSCRIBERS. Recent scholarly interest in this topic has been considerable. Inevitably, the researcher examining early editions will be fascinated by such convenient listings of those persons who are known to have been active supporters of the composer, and who were probably among the first to hear the music. The lists may also help in dating, both through specific names that they contain, and as a suggestion that the scholar may want to scan contemporary journals for advanced notice of the subscription. The date of such announcements, also the names in the list itself, offer a *terminus post quem* for the publication date.

NOTES: Klaus Hortschansky, "Pränumerations- und Subskriptionsliste im Notendrucken deutscher Musiker des 18. Jahrhunderts," *Acta musicologica,* 40 (1968), 154–74, includes many useful references to early lists and related documents as well as to recent studies.

The British Museum possesses a card index of "Subscribers' lists found in musical publications from 1711 to c.1860, to a total of 218 cards. Most of the lists are British: there are some 30 cards for other European countries."[107]

1.   The presence of a subscription list in a particular copy is evidence of a copy that is similar to or closely related to the earliest copy; and in the absence of any evidence to the contrary, the date of publication should be assumed to be the date of this particular copy. The absence of a subscription list in a particular copy of an edition known to have once included such a list may indicate either that the copy is from a late impression, or merely that the subscription list has been removed.

2.   Occasionally a partial list of subscribers appears in one copy, with a fuller list in a later copy.

EXAMPLES:

1.   The Pleyel edition of the "complete" Haydn quartets exists in three states: First, with a type-set list of subscribers extending alphabetically only from A to N (a date of 1802 has been suggested); second, with the same list extended to include notable and royal names, including "S.M. l'Empereur-Roi à Vienne" (Napoleon assumed the title on 18 May 1804, which is a *terminus post quem* for this state: a date of 1805 has been suggested); and third, with the complete list, lithographed (a date of 1810 has been suggested).[108]

2.   The deterioration of a list in the course of serial publication is illustrated in the case of the Handel edition of Dr. Arnold.[109]

E.   SALES AND OWNERSHIP.

1.   *"Control numbers," "control signatures," and their equivalents.* These provided the composer with a marking through which he could detect copies which the publisher had printed above and beyond the number agreed to.[110] The presence of such evidence indicates a copy from the earliest authorized press run; hence, the publication date of the edition is the date of the copy. (A control signature may be seen in Figure 81.)

NOTE: Such numbers, according to Deutsch, "occurred more frequently in England than on the Continent. Schubert availed himself of this check and made such indications (number and signature, or initials) usually on the last page of his books. . . . In England also it is the custom of publishers to sign their names on music; at first it was done in manuscript and later with rubber [i.e., metal or wood?] stamps. Manuscript signatures were, however, used in France even earli-

107

(E.) er in the 18th century. Haydn stamped the copies of *Die Schöpfung,* published in 1800 by himself, with his initials (without Control Numbers). English composers, since the second half of the 19th century, used rubber stamps with their signatures. Control numbers, however, are found occasionally on English music; e.g., Edward Smith Brigg's *Here's a health to those far away* (Robert Birchall, *ca.*1796 [watermark 1794] and later), signed, with initials, and numbered in more than 2,700 copies."[111]

2. *Prices and Currency.* The price of music, as specified on the title page, can be useful in two ways.

a. The names of currency units can often be assigned to specific inclusive dates.

EXAMPLE: German music before 1837/38 was priced in Gröschen; after 1837/38, in Neugröschen.

NOTES: For the names of the currency used on the music of various countries, see the National Reports below, item K.

Among the various guides to coins and currency, the following have been particularly useful in the present study:

William D. Craig, *Coins of the World, 1750—1850* (Racine, Wisconsin 1966).

Albert R. Frey, *Dictionary of Numismatic Names* (New York 1917, 1947).

Burton Hobson & Robert Obojski, *Illustrated Encyclopedia of World Coins* (New York 1970).

b. Changes in price, because of rising costs, inflation, greater or less demand for a particular edition, or the like, often serve to identify new issues of an edition. Ideally the exact date of the change should be verified in contemporary announcements, although such verification may be impossible.

EXAMPLES:

1. The Breitkopf & Härtel edition of Beethoven's trios, op.70 (1809), was originally priced at 2 Rthlr. and then changed to 1 Rthlr. 12 Gr. The second issue may be seen in two states: first, with the price altered in manuscript (in the Hoboken collection), and second, with the new price re-struck on the plates (in the Hirsch collection).[112]

2. The Simrock vocal score of Mozart's *Le nozze di Figaro* (1796) exists in four states, described in Fuld, p. 293.

c. The price announced on an edition or in a list was not necessarily the price at which the music was sold, or even at which it was expected to be sold. The practice of selling at half price, which Kidson speaks of,[113] was probably widespread. Unfortunately, but understandably, the evidence in such matters is very incomplete.

d. The cost can occasionally be used to estimate how much of an incomplete edition is lost. For example, much American sheet music in the early 19th century was priced at 12-1/2 cents per sheet (a sheet including either one or two printed pages). An incomplete edition of four pages, priced at 37-1/2 cents, is probably lacking one sheet. Unfortunately, such simple rules become less consistently applicable to larger and more ambitious editions.

3. *Stamps of Publishers or Dealers.* These consist of several different kinds, which may be distinguished as follows:

a. Publishers' stamps, such as the blind embossed designs used by Ricordi in recent years. Deutsch has described several of the different types and appearances.[114]

b. Dealers' stamps. These have not been collected or studied, although the form of the name and the address on the stamp can probably aid in determining the date when the music was offered for sale, which is a *terminus ante quem* for the date of the edition. Frequently the "stamp" is a small-size engraving added to the title page. When Werckmeister succeeded Zulehner, for instance, he used small oblong plates to mark the Zulehner editions.

c. Paste-over labels, which cover the original imprint. These pose a special problem: does the new imprint indicate a new publisher or merely a dealer? (See, for examples, Figures 8 and 12.) Which should be used to determine a date, the label or the undersurface? As general rules, the following appear to be appropriate:

i. When the label identifies a publisher who is known to have succeeded the publisher named in the original imprint, or to have acquired some of his stock, use the publisher named on the label.

ii. When the label identifies a firm which acted only as a dealer, or when there is no evidence that this firm ever succeeded or acquired plates from the original publisher, use the original publisher.

iii. When in doubt, use the original publisher.

(E.3.c.) iv. In every instance, identify both the label and the under-surface.

4. *Evidence of ownership.* Manuscript signatures and stamps of owners, anecdotal information, personal bindings, and bookplates often suggest a useful *terminus ante quem* for the date of publication.

a. Ownership signatures only rarely give the date, which may be that either of the purchase or of the inscription. While such owners are not generally among the most reliable of historical sources, there seems to be no reason to question the credibility of their statements unless this evidence conflicts with other evidence. Nonetheless, dated inscriptions remain interesting mostly as evidence of the dissemination of a work. Bookplates are likewise useful; they are occasionally dated, but usually with a date of purchase or cataloguing, or sometimes with the date of the engraving of the book plate itself, but not likely the date of publication.

> EXAMPLE: An owner's signature may be seen in Figure 81. In the latter, the signature at the top is that of the owner; the one near the first musical system is a composer's control number (see VII.E.1. above).

b. Among the occasional accounts found in diaries, letters, and personal accounts is the happy story of William Gardiner telling of his visit to Pleyel's shop in Paris where he saw the new edition of Haydn's string quartets. "The copy I got was the first he sold."[115] Unfortunately, we do not know exactly when in 1802 Gardiner visited Paris. Furthermore, Gardiner has a rather poor reputation as to accuracy.

c. Personal binding styles went through various fashions, so that contemporary bindings suggest approximate dates. Of the various binding styles used for music, the most distinctive is the green parchment used in 18th-century France. Small red leather labels, on the spine or the front cover, usually bear the name of the work or the owner heavily stamped in gold. The edges are typically colored, almost always red before 1795 and almost always yellow thereafter. Three-quarters or half-parchment bindings with cream-colored parchment and paste paper covers, mostly in blue, were particularly common in the early 19th century. Publishers' cloth binding dates from around 1825, but its use for music volumes has yet to be studied and dated.

5. *Travel time.* In Europe during the period of this study, travel was reasonably fast (a matter of days or at most weeks) from one city to another, although not always dependable. Travel from Europe to the Western Hemisphere generally took about two months, but was impossible in the winter. Thus an American piracy of a London comic opera tune, first presented in London in March 1805, could have been printed in Boston in 1805; whereas an opera first presented in November 1805 could not have been pirated in Boston before 1806. Because of the complicated arrangements often made among composers, publishers, and agents, travel time should not be considered when estimating dates, except in the light of specific facts relating to the edition in question.

F. PUBLISHED CATALOGUES AND BIBLIOGRAPHICAL LISTS. In the course of his studies, the scholar will come to use reference works, such as library catalogues, composer lists (including our venerable thematic catalogues), and surveys of particular repertories. Dates in these sources should be accepted only after the following matters have been taken into consideration.

1. How reliable is the list? Who prepared it, and when? Is information provided or implied which tells how the date was arrived at?

2. Is the copy described likely to be similar to the one at hand; or, if the publication date is needed, is the copy described likely to be identical to the earliest copy? Conversely, if publication dates are given, can the date of publication be accepted as the date of a copy at hand (see I.E.2. above)?

Authorities Cited

1. William C. Smith, *Handel: A Descriptive Catalogue of the Early Editions,* 2nd ed. (Oxford 1970), p. 248.

2. Anthony van Hoboken, "Probleme der musikbibliographischen Terminologie," *Fontes artis musicae,* 5 (1958), 7.

3. On the authority of Rudolf Elvers.

4. See, for instance, the observation by Sir Jack Westrup that "The conventional language of bibliography is inadequate" to a situation under discussion: *Music and Letters,* 48 (1967), 312; as well as the response by Alan Tyson, pp. 412—3.

5. Paul Hirsch, "Some Early Mozart Editions," *Music Review,* 1 (1940), 55—6.

6. D.W. Krummel, *English Music Printing, 1553—1700* (London, forthcoming).

7. William C. Smith, *Concerning Handel* (London 1948), p. 77.

8. Cecil Hopkinson, *A Bibliographical Thematic Catalogue of the Works of John Field, 1782—1837* (London 1961), p. 13.

9. P.H. Muir, "Thomas Moore's Irish Melodies," *The Colophon,* 15 (1933).

10. Richard J. Wolfe, *Secular Music in America, 1801—1825* (New York 1964), item 8329-B. See also Joseph Muller, *The Star Spangled Banner* (New York 1935), pp. 52—7, as well as the facsimile in Harry Dichter, *Musical Americana's One Hundred Great American Songs* (Philadelphia 1956—7).

11. Otto Erich Deutsch, "The First Editions of Brahms," *Music Review,* 1 (1940), 131.

12. Michael Tilmouth, "A Note on the Cost of Music Printing in London in 1702," *Brio,* 8 (1971), 1—3.

13. Otto Erich Deutsch, "Mozarts Verleger," *Mozart Jahrbuch,* 1955, p. 50.

14. Alan Tyson, "Steps to Publication — and Beyond," in *The Beethoven Companion* (London 1971), pp. 474—5.

15. Georg Kinsky & Hans Halm, *Das Werk Beethovens* (Munich, Duisburg 1955), p. 222.

16. *Tradition und Gegenwart: Festschrift zum 150-jährigen Bestehen des Musikverlags Friedrich Hofmeister* (Leipzig 1957), p. 10.

17. Kathi Meyer, "Was sind musikalische Erstausgaben?," *Philobiblon,* 8 (1935), 183.

18. On the authority of Dan Fog.

19. Both copies are listed in Richard Macnutt, *Catalogue 103,* items 122—3.

20. Cecil Hopkinson, *A Bibliography of the Works of C.W. von Gluck, 1714—1787* (London 1959), p. 40, introductory comments; items 44A and 44A[b].

21. Both copies are listed in Richard Macnutt, *Catalogue 103,* items 86—7.

22. Copy 1 is in the British Museum: Hirsch II., 133. Copy 2 is listed in Richard Macnutt, *Catalogue 103,* item 187. Copy 3 is listed in the *British Union-Catalogue of Early Music* (London 1957), p. 186; also in O.G. Sonneck's Library of Congress *Dramatic Music: Catalogue of Full Scores* (Washington 1908), p. 32.

23. Kinsky & Halm, p. 186.

24. Copy 1 appears in the *British Union-Catalogue,* p. 635, and Sonneck, p. 100. Copy 2 is listed in H. Baron, *Catalogue 91,* item 140.

25. Cecil Hopkinson, "Notes on the Earliest Editions of Gounod's Faust," *Festschrift Otto Erich Deutsch* (Kassel 1963), pp. 246–7.

26. Copy 1 is listed in William C. Smith, *A Bibliography of the Musical Works Published by John Walsh during the Years 1695–1720* (London 1948), p. 79, item 246; copy 2 is item 254.

27. Kinsky & Halm, p. 64.

28. Richard Macnutt, *Catalogue 103,* item 22.

29. Smith, *Handel: A Descriptive Catalogue,* pp. 248–9.

30. See Alan Tyson, "Mozart's Piano Sonatas," *Musical Times,* 107 (1966), 888.

31. Geneviève Thibault, "Note sur une édition inconnue de Clérambault," *Revue de musicologie,* 52 (1966), 210–11.

32. See, however, Kenneth Gilbert, "Les Livres de Clavéçin de François Couperin," *Revue de musicologie,* 58 (1972), 256–61.

33. Paul Hirsch, "More Early Mozart Editions," *Music Review,* 3 (1942), 38–41.

34. *Catalogue of Printed Music, Accessions, Part 53: Music in the Hirsch Library* (London 1951), p. 69.

35. See, for instance, the British Museum's collection from c.1695 entitled *Joyful Cuckoldom: British Union-Catalogue,* p. 561.

36. Cecil Hopkinson, *Tannhäuser: An Examination of 36 Editions* (Tutzing 1973).

37. For similar examples, see Hans Schneider, "Zur Datierung der Musikdrucke des Verlages B. Schotts Söhne," *Aus dem Antiquariat,* 27 (1971), A32–6; also Cari Johansson, *J.J. & B. Hummel* (Stockholm 1972), v. 1, pp. 79–117.

38. The practice of "hyphenated numbers" in American Midwestern editions around 1850 is discussed in Ernst Krohn, *Music Publishing in the Middle Western States* (Detroit 1972), pp. 32–4.

39. Smith, *A Bibliography of . . . John Walsh . . . , 1695–1720,* p. xxiii; also Smith and Charles Humphries, *A Bibliography of . . . John Walsh . . . , 1721–1766* (London 1968), p. xiv.

40. Donald W. Krummel, *Philadelphia Music Engraving and Publishing* (Ann Arbor 1958), p. 126; Wolfe, *Secular Music in America,* pp 1183–7. In Wolfe's index, p. 1161, most numbers with an "A" suffix refer to the latter of two such states.

41. Cecil Hopkinson, *A Bibliography of the Musical and Literary Works of Hector Berlioz, 1803–1869* (Edinburgh 1951), p. 48, items 25A and 25A(*a*).

42. On the authority of Rudolf Elvers.

43. Hopkinson, *Berlioz,* pp. xvi, 117, 125.

44. Wolfgang Matthäus, "Quellen und Fehlerquellen zur Datierung von Musikdrucke aus der Zeit nach 1750," *Fontes artis musicae,* 14 (1967), 38.

45. Kinsky & Halm, p. 66. The later edition is in the Newberry Library, 8A 1859.

46. Kinsky & Halm, p. 312.

47. Hopkinson, *Berlioz,* p. xvi.

48. Rudolf Steglich, 'Zwei Titelzeichnungen zu Robert Schumanns Jugendalbum als Interpretationsdokumente," *Deutsches Jahrbuch der Musikwissenschaft,* 4 (1959), 38–9, 47.

49. James J. Fuld, *The Book of World-Famous Music,* 2nd ed. (New York 1971), p. 320.

50. Alexander Weinmann, *Vollständiges Verlagsverzeichnis Artaria & Comp.* (Vienna 1952; Beiträge zur Geschichte des Alt-Wiener Musikverlages, Reihe 2, Folge 2), p. 163.

51. Fuld, p. 69; see also Cecil Hopkinson, *A Bibliography of the Works of Giuseppe Verdi,* v. 1 (New York 1973), p. 93.

52. Otto Erich Deutsch, *Musikverlagsnummern* (Berlin 1961), p. 9.

53. Matthäus, "Quellen und Fehlerquellen," pp. 38—9.

54. Hoboken, "Probleme," p. 13.

55. J.M. Coopersmith, "The First *Gesamtausgabe:* Dr. Arnold's Edition of Handel's Works," Music Library Association *Notes,* II, 4 (1947), 288.

56. Johansson, *J.J. & B. Hummel,* vol. 1, pp. 10—11.

57. O.W. Neighbour & Alan Tyson, *English Music Publishers' Plate Numbers in the First Half of the Nineteenth Century* (London 1965), p. 12.

58. Hopkinson, *Field, passim.*

59. Johansson, *J.J. & B. Hummel,* vol. 1, p. 89. See also the National Reports below, II.D.: Hummel.

60. Neighbour & Tyson, p. 12.

61. Krummel, *Philadelphia Music Engraving and Publishing,* pp. 119—21; Wolfe, *Secular Music in America,* pp. 1181—3.

62. Hopkinson, *Field,* p. 164.

63. Hoboken, "Probleme," p. 12.

64. H. Baron, *Catalogue 91,* item 95.

65. Weinmann, *Artaria,* pp. 20—1.

66. Alexander Weinmann, *Die Wiener Verlagswerke von Franz Anton Hoffmeister* (Vienna 1964; Beiträge zur Geschichte des Alt-Wiener Musikverlages, Reihe 2, Folge 8), pp. 213—5, 233—5.

67. On the authority of Alan Tyson.

68. Hopkinson, *Berlioz,* p. 77, item 36D(*g*).

69. Alexander Weinmann, *Verlagsverzeichnis Giovanni Cappi bis A.O. Witzendorf* (Vienna 1967; Beiträge zur Geschichte des Alt-Wiener Musikverlages, Reihe 2, Folge 11), p. 118.

70. On the basis of information kindly supplied by William Lichtenwanger and Wilbur Jones of the Library of Congress.

71. On the authority of Hermann Baron.

72. Cecil Hopkinson, *A Dictionary of Parisian Music Publishers, 1700—1950* (London 1954), p. 13.

73. Krummel, *Philadelphia Music Engraving and Publishing,* pp. 106—7.

74. Matthäus, "Quellen und Fehlerquellen," p. 39.

75. Kinsky & Halm, p. 312.

76. Deutsch, "The First Editions of Brahms," p. 265.

77. Maurice J.E. Brown, *Chopin: An Index of His Works in Chronological Order* (2nd ed.; New York 1972), p. 63.

78. Steglich, "Zwei Titelzeichnungen," facing p. 40.

79. On the authority of Philip Gossett.

80. D.W. Krummel, "Late 18th Century French Music Publishers' Catalogs in the Library of Congress," *Fontes artis musicae,* 7 (1960), 64.

81. Bohdan Muchenberg, "Z zagadnién dokumentacji symfonii polskiej drugiej połowy XVIII wieku," *Z dziejów muzyki polskiej,* 14 (1969), 65–85; also the reviews by B.E. Wilson, *Journal of the American Musicological Society,* 21 (1968), 400–4, and D.W. Krummel, Music Library Association *Notes,* II, 24 (1968), 697–700.

82. Gwilym Beechey, "Carl Friedrich Abel's Six Symphonies, op.14," *Music and Letters,* 51 (1970), 280–1.

83. "Watermarks and Musicology," *Acta Musicologica,* 33 (1961), 127.

84. On the authority of Dan Fog.

85. Tyson, "Steps to Publication," p. 484.

86. Smith, *Handel: A Descriptive Catalogue,* p. 261.

87. "The First Editions of Brahms," p. 129.

88. Recorded in the S.A.E. Hagen record books in Copenhagen (see the National Reports, XV:F.), reported by Dan Fog.

89. Julius Grant, *Books and Documents: Dating, Permanence, and Preservation* (London 1937), pp. 43–4.

90. Liesbeth Weinhold, "Musiktitel und Datierung," *Fontes artis musicae,* 13 (1966), 136–40; Wolfgang Matthäus, "Die Elemente des Titelblattes im 18. Jahrhundert," *Fontes artis musicae,* 12 (1965), 23–6.

91. "Music Bibliography and Catalogues," *The Library,* IV, 23 (1943), 159–61.

92. The quotation is from Deutsch's "Music and Bibliographical Practice," *Music Review,* 2 (1941), 253, 256.

93. Smith, *Concerning Handel,* p. 74.

94. *J.J. & B. Hummel,* vol. 1, p. 111.

95. Deutsch, "Music and Bibliographical Practice," p. 255.

96. On the authority of Dan Fog.

97. Deutsch, "The First Editions of Brahms," p. 140.

98. Krummel, *Philadelphia Music Engraving and Publishing,* pp. 73–92, 98–143, which is partly duplicated in "Graphic Analysis," Music Library Association *Notes,* II, 16 (1959), 213–33, which, however, also contains additional information.

99. "Music and Bibliographical Practice," pp. 254–5.

100. Weinhold, "Musiktitel und Datierung," p. 137.

101. Philip Gossett, *The Operas of Rossini: Problems of Textual Criticism in Nineteenth-Century Opera* (Princeton 1970), p. 570.

102. Gossett, p. 566.

103. Alan Tyson, *Thematic Catalogue of the Works of Muzio Clementi* (Tutzing 1967), pp. 82–3.

104. "Steps to Publication," pp. 484–6.

105. "Was sind musikalische Erstausgaben?," *Philobiblon,* 8 (1935), 181–4.

106.   An extensive listing of German materials is found in Hans-Martin Plesske, "Bibliographie des Schrifttums zur Geschichte deutscher und österreichischer Musikverlage," *Beiträge zur Geschichte des Buchwesens,* 3 (1968), 135–222.

107.   A. Hyatt King, "The History and Growth of the Catalogues in the Music Room of the British Museum," *Festschrift Otto Erich Deutsch* (Kassel 1963), p. 308.

108.   Otto Erich Deutsch, "Theme and Variations," *Music Review,* 12 (1951), 70–71.

109.   Coopersmith, "The First *Gesamtausgabe,"* p. 288.

110.   Georg Kinsky, "Signierte Schubert-Erstdrucke," *Philobiblon,* 4 (1931), 183–8.

111.   "Music Bibliography and Catalogues," p. 164.

112.   Kinsky & Halm, pp. 167–8.

113.   Frank Kidson, *British Music Publishers* (London 1900), p. 134.

114.   "Music Bibliography and Catalogues," p. 153n.

115.   William Gardiner, *Music and Friends* (London 1838), pp. 262–3.

116

Selected List of Writings

This list contains the publications which are concerned with the study of printed musical editions as physical objects (rather than with the description and organization of music in bibliographical lists), and which are regarded today as the important presentations of new techniques and viewpoints, or as the most important discussions of the entire field as a survey. Studies of particular topics, which are cited in the text of this book, are included here only insofar as they are concerned with and important in the development of the theory of music bibliography in general. The arrangement is chronological.

1914. William Barclay Squire, "Publisher's Numbers," *Sammelbände der Internationalen Musikgesellschaft,* 15 (1914), 420–7.

1927. Otto Erich Deutsch, "Über die bibliographische Aufnahme von Originalausgaben unserer Klassiker," *Beethoven Zentenarfeier . . . : Internationaler Musikhistorischer Kongress* (Wien 1927), pp. 268–72.

——. Josef Schmidt-Phiseldeck, "Datierung der Musikalien," *ibid.,* pp. 279–82.

1929. Kathi Meyer, "Über Musikbibliographie," *Musikwissenschaftliche Beiträge; Festschrift für Johannes Wolf* (Berlin 1929), pp. 118–22.

1931–6. Georg Kinsky, articles in *Philobiblon:* "Signierte Schubert-Erstdrucke," 4 (1931), 183–8; "Erstlingsdrucke der deutschen Tonmeister der Klassik und Romantik," 7 (1934), 347–66; "Die Urschriften Bachs und Händels," 8 (1935), 109–22; "Berühmte Opern, ihre Handschriften und Erstdrucken," 8 (1935), 363–94; "Die Erstausgaben und Handschriften der Sinfonien Beethovens," 9 (1936), 339–51.

1934. C.B. Oldman, "Collecting Musical First Editions," in John Carter, *New Paths in Book Collecting* (London 1934), pp. 95–124. Also issued separately with addenda and corrigenda (London 1938; Aspects of Book-Collecting.).

1935. Kathi Meyer, "Was sind musikalische Erstausgaben?," *Philobiblon,* 8 (1935), 181–4.

1938. Richard S. Hill, "The Plate Numbers of C.F. Peters' Predecessors," *Papers of the American Musicological Society,* 1 (1938), 113–34.

1940. Otto Erich Deutsch, "The First Editions of Brahms," *Music Review*, 1 (1940), 123–43, 255–78, especially pp. 128–31.

1941. Otto Erich Deutsch, "Music and Bibliographical Practice," *ibid.*, 2 (1941), 253–6.

1943. Otto Erich Deutsch, "Music Bibliography and Catalogues," *The Library*, IV, 23 (1943), 151–70.

1946. Otto Erich Deutsch, "Music Publishers' Numbers: A Selection of 40 Dated Lists, 1710–1900," *Journal of Documentation*, 1 (1946), 206–16; 2 (1946), 80–91, also issued separately (London 1946); 2nd ed., expanded, as *Musikverlagsnummern* (Berlin 1961).

1951. Cecil Hopkinson, *A Bibliography of the Musical and Literary Works of Hector Berlioz, (1803–1869), with Histories of the French Music Publishers Concerned* (Edinburgh 1951), especially pp. xii–xviii.

1951. Otto Erich Deutsch, "Theme and Variations," *Music Review*, 12 (1951), 68–71.

1954. Cari Johansson, "Publishers' Addresses as a Guide to the Dating of French Printed Music of the Second Half of the Eighteenth Century," *Fontes artis musicae*, 1 (1954), 14–9.

1955. Cecil Hopkinson, "Fundamentals of Music Bibliography," *Journal of Documentation*, 11 (1955), 119–29.

1958. Anthony van Hoboken, "Probleme der musikbibliographischen Terminologie," *Fontes artis musicae*, 5 (1958), 6–15.

1959. Donald W. Krummel, "Graphic Analysis: Its Application to Early American Engraved Music," Music Library Association *Notes*, II, 16 (1959), 213–33.

1959. "Toward a Definition of Certain Terms in Music Bibliography," in *Music, Libraries, and Instruments* (London 1961; Hinrichsen's 11th Music Book), pp. 147–55. [Report on a session, organized by Cecil Hopkinson, at the Congress of the International Association of Music Libraries, Cambridge 1959.]

1963. Alan Tyson, *The Authentic English Editions of Beethoven* (London 1963; All Souls Studies.).

1965. Wolfgang Matthäus, "Die Elemente des Titelblattes im 18. Jahrhundert," *Fontes artis musicae*, 12 (1965), 23–6.

1966. Liesbeth Weinhold, "Musiktitel und Datierung," *Fontes artis musicae,* 13 (1966), 136–40.

1966. James J. Fuld, "Introduction" to *The Book of World-Famous Music* (New York 1966), pp. 3–70; 2nd ed. (New York 1971), pp. 3–81.

1967. Wolfgang Matthäus, "Quellen und Fehlerquellen zur Datierung von Musikdrucken aus der Zeit nach 1750," *Fontes artis musicae,* 14 (1967), 37–42.

1970. Claudio Sartori, "The Bibliographer's Occupation," Music Library Association *Notes,* II, 26 (1970), 705–12.

1971. Hans Lenneberg, "Dating Engraved Music: The Present State of the Art," *Library Quarterly,* 41 (1971), 128–40.

Glossary of Terms

COUNTERPARTS AND REFERENCES

The most important technical terms used in this study, in English, French, and German, are listed below. In the column marked "Code" are references to the relevant sections of the International Association of Music Libraries' *Rules for Full Cataloging,* compiled by Virginia Cunningham (Frankfurt 1971; Code International de Catalogage de la musique, III.). The far right column refers to the section of the Synopsis above in which these terms are defined or discussed. Whenever possible, the terms in the present *Guide* have been defined so as to conform to the definitions in the "Glossary of Terms" (pp. 73–111) of the *Code.* Differences arise insofar as the objectives of bibliography and of cataloguing may differ.

English	French	German	Code	Synopsis
Edition	Édition	Ausgabe	—	I.D.1
Issue	Publication[1]	Auflage[1]	—	I.D.2
State	État[1]	Variant[1]	—	I.D.3
Impression	Tirage[1]	Abzug[1]	—	I.D.4
Plate number	Cotage	Plattennummer	3.47	II.
Publisher's number	Cotage (Numero d'édition)	Verlagsnummer	3.47	II.
Imprint	Adresse bibliographique	Erscheinungsvermerk	3.4	III.
Selling agent	Dépositaire	Auslieferungsfirmen	3.44	III.C.
Caption title	Titre de départ	Kopftitel	3.111	I.D.2.a.i.(1.)
Cover title	Titre de couverture	Umschlagtitel	3.111	I.D.2.a.i.(4.)

[1] See the discussion of terminology in I.D.5.e.

Composite edition	Édition composite	Zusammengesetzte Auflage	2.4	I.D.2.
Extract	Extrait	Ausschnitt	2.4	I.D.2.
Legal deposit	Dépôt legal	Pflichtablieferung		IV.
Watermark	Filigrane	Wasserzeichen		VI.C.
Publisher's label	Collette	Verlagsetikett	3.44	VII.C.1.a.

National Reports

Figure 44: A LONDON MUSIC SHOP, c.1825. On each window is displayed the title of an edition for sale in the shop. Another depiction of Mayhew's shop, on this same musical work, is seen in Doreen & Sidney Spellman, *Victorian Music Covers* (Park Ridge, New Jersey, 1972), facing p. 70. (The difference in the two lithographs is attested by the "catalogue" of titles shown in the windows, also by the alignment of the word "Old" in relation to "Co." beneath it.) This particular song (better known today as, "Ach, du lieber Augustin") came to be a favorite one for illustrating music shops. For a view of Mori & Lavenu's, see Neighbour & Tyson, *front.*; for citations of several on American editions, see Dichter & Shapiro, pp. 87–91.

Prospectus

In 1968 the Editor prepared a list of questions, which was then sent to scholars specializing in the music bibliography of various countries or geographical areas. The scholars selected were, whenever possible, native to these areas. Generally the response was prompt and ample, but inevitably difficulties occurred. In some instances, no scholars could be located; in other instances, the only specialists who could be identified were too busy with other commitments. When these situations occurred, the National Reports were prepared by the Editor, often with assistance, as noted below.

The twelve questions (re-worded somewhat for the purposes of this book) became the sub-headings for the National Reports which follow:

A. SUMMARIES AND BIBLIOGRAPHIES: Are there books or articles which provide a general history of the music published in this particular geographical area, or in any of its subdivisions or cities? Also, are there any bibliographies — comprehensive or selective — which list the musical editions published in the area? Are there writings about these editions?

B. DIRECTORIES: Are there lists of music publishers, printers, engravers, or dealers? Do any general directories list their names? (Included here are both contemporary sources and modern scholarly compilations.)

C. IMPORTANT NAMES: Who were the important publishers, printers, and engravers of music? When were they active; why are they important; and what are the modern studies of their work? (References to any illustrations of their work which are reproduced in this study are indicated here.)

> NOTE: Several countries are privileged to have reference books containing detailed entries for the music trade (e.g., Hopkinson for France, Dichter and Shapiro for the United States). Although selective lists for such countries might appear to be superfluous, they are useful to the novice, as a means of familiarization with those names most likely to be encountered. Where there is a modern reference

guide to the music trade — such as would be listed under B. — the scholar should of course be expected to consult it for more extensive information. The dates quoted, for the most part those cited in various directories, do not necessarily reflect the publishing career of the man or the firm. Often a man managed a music shop for many years before he began publishing; and often he gradually gave up publishing some time before he died or before his shop closed or was sold. Any better chronology of music publishing, however, must depend on better dating — which of course is the objective of this book.

D. PLATE NUMBERS: Did publishers ever use plate numbers? If so, are there published lists or card files which provide an inventory of musical editions containing plate numbers?

NOTE: The work of the Commission for Bibliographical Research, it will be remembered, began as an attempt to collect plate numbers. The result of this early work was presented in the article, "Cotages d'éditeurs à c.1850: Liste préliminaire," *Fontes artis musicae,* 14 (1967), 22–37. The lists of plate numbers presented in this article have been largely incorporated or updated in the present book.

E. CATALOGUES: Are there any early lists of music for sale by publishers or dealers (either separate lists or added "plate catalogues")?

F. COPYRIGHT: 1. When was music first copyrighted or registered? 2. In what form does the statement of copyright typically appear on the music? 3. Are there any records (official or unofficial, published or in manuscript) of all the music copyrighted or registered? 4. Are there extant depository copies, in one library or scattered; and how can these copies be identified?

G. ANNOUNCEMENTS: Are there publications, such as newspapers or journals, which are particularly valuable for advertisements of newly published music? Have their entries been extracted and indexed, either in published form or on cards?

H. DESIGN AND PRINTING PRACTICE: Are there any studies, completed or in progress, concerned with the styles and the processes of music printing?

J. PAPER: Are there any studies, completed or in progress, concerned with the watermarks which have been or might be found in musical editions?

K. UNITS OF CURRENCY AND PRICING PRACTICES: What were the units of coinage, and what were their relationships? Did these change between 1700 and 1860? Were there any special practices in the pricing of music that are known?

L. IMPORTANT COLLECTIONS: Which libraries, public and private, have important collections of the music published in the geographical area? Have any collections been assembled for the specific purpose of studying this music? (Identified by RISM sigla.)

M. OTHER EVIDENCE: Are there any other kinds of evidence which are useful in dating and studying the musical editions in question?

The National Reports are arranged in a succession so as generally to reflect the sequence of the origins of music publishing in various countries after 1700, i.e., from England across to the Low Countries, down into southern Europe, up into central and across into eastern Europe, back through northern Europe, and finally to the Western Hemisphere.

Almand

EARLY ENGLISH ENGRAVINGS.
Figure 45 (left): Keyboard music, 1696, re-issued in 1705. *Figure 46 (lower left)*: Song sheet, c.1710. *Figure 47 (lower right)*: Song sheet, c.1730.

I. *Great Britain*

A. HYATT KING, O.W. NEIGHBOUR, & ALAN TYSON

A. SUMMARIES: The best general survey appears in the introduction, pp. 13–37, to Charles Humphries & William C. Smith, *Music Publishing in the British Isles* (London 1954; 2nd ed, 1970). Various dating methods are discussed in detail in O.W. Neighbour & Alan Tyson, *English Music Publishers' Plate Numbers in the First Half of the Nineteenth Century* (London 1965), pp. 9–16.

B. DIRECTORIES: The coverage in Humphries & Smith extends "from the earliest times to the middle of the nineteenth century." It largely supersedes Frank Kidson's *British Music Publishers, Printers and Engravers* (London 1900), as well as his articles in the second edition of *Grove's Dictionary*.

C. IMPORTANT NAMES (all in London unless otherwise indicated):

Thomas **Cross**, c.1685–c.1733.

John **Walsh**, c.1696–1736; John Walsh II, 1736–1766. See William C. Smith, *A Bibliography of the Musical Works published by John Walsh during the Years 1695–1720* (London 1948); also William C. Smith & Charles Humphries, *A Bibliography of the Musical Works published by the Firm of John Walsh during the Years 1721–1766* (London 1968); also the same compilers' *Handel: A Descriptive Catalogue of the Early Editions* (London 1960; 2nd ed, 1970). See Figures 32–36, 46, 48–51, 56.

Richard **Meares**, father & son, c.1700–1743.

John **Cluer**, 1715–1728. See Figure 52.

Benjamin **Cooke**, 1726–1743. See Figure 53.

John **Simpson**, 1734–c.1749; later his heirs, including John **Cox**, 1751–1764.

John **Johnson**, c.1740–1777. See Figures 55, 57.

The **Thompson** family, Peter, Charles, Samuel, Ann, Peter II, and Henry, c.1750–1805. See Figure 61.

Robert **Bremner**, c.1760–1789 (also in Edinburgh). See Figure 59.

Peter **Welcker**, 1762–1775; later his heirs, including John Welcker.

William **Forster**, father & son, c.1762–1824.

Randall & Abell, 1766–1783.

James **Longman**, later his son John, c.1767–1822, with various partners, notably as **Longman & Broderip**, 1776–1798, and **Longman & Clementi**, 1798–c.1801. See Figures 60, 67.

William **Napier**, c.1772–1791.

John **Preston**, c.1774–c.1798; his son Thomas, c.1798–1834.

John **Bland**, c.1776–1795. See Figures 62–3, 68.

John **Johnston**, 1767–1778 (not to be confused with John Johnson above). See Figure 64.

The **Corri** family, including Domenico, John, Natale, & Montague, c.1779–1822 (active in Edinburgh & London); with various partners, e.g., as Corri & **Dussek**, 1794–c.1801.

Robert **Birchall**, 1783–1819, with various partners, e.g., as Birchall & Andrews; later as Lonsdale & Mills (below). See Figure 66.

Joseph **Dale**, 1783–1821.

George **Goulding**, Later Goulding, d'Almaine, &c., c.1786–1834. See Figure 77.

Theobald **Monzani**, with various partners, 1787–c.1829. See Figure 65.

Nathaniel **Gow**, later Gow & Shepard, 1788–1827 (in Edinburgh).

The **Hime** family, c.1790–c.1835 (active mostly in Dublin).

George **Walker**, c.1790–1848, with various partners (in Edinburgh). See Figure 72.

WALSH EDITIONS. *Figure 48 (upper left)*: Harpsichord suites, 1715. *Figure 49 (upper right)*: Instrumental parts, 1730. *Figure 50 (lower left)*: Operatic aria, 1730. *Figure 51 (lower right)*: Oratorio score, 1743.

Lewis **Lavenu**, and heirs, c.1796–1844; Lavenu & Mitchell, c.1802–1808.

Francis **Broderip**, after partnership with Longman (above), as Broderip & Wilkinson, 1798–1808; **Wilkinson** & Co., 1808–c.1810. See Figure 70.

Muzio **Clementi**, after partnership with Longman (above), as Clementi, Collard, Banger, Hyde, & Davis, which eventually became Collard & Collard, c.1830–1834.

The **Power** brothers, William, 1802–1831 (in Dublin) and James, c.1807–1838 (in London).

Chappell & Co., with various partners, founded 1811. See Figures 7–11, 71, 78.

Vincent **Novello**, founded 1811. See *A Short History of Cheap Music* (London 1887); also *150 Years in Soho* (London 1961).

Isaac **Willis**, c.1816–1862 (in Dublin & London).

Thomas **Boosey**, founded c.1814. See Figure 73.

Johann Baptist **Cramer**, with various partners, founded 1824.

Christopher **Lonsdale** & Richard **Mills**, formerly with Birchall (above), 1829–1834, separately thereafter. See Figure 76.

Wessel & Co., c.1838–1860, previously as Wessel & Stodart.

Joseph **Williams**, founded 1844.

For further information, see Humphries & Smith.

D. PLATE NUMBERS: Dated lists are given in Neighbour & Tyson. Plate numbers were seldom used in Great Britain before the nineteenth century. Walsh used publishers' numbers, but they are not reliable for dating. Dates for Walsh editions, based mostly on announcements, can in any case be found in the Smith bibliographies.

E. CATALOGUES: Many publishers issued plate catalogues, some of which are several pages long. In addition are several separately issued lists. Most of these are cited in Humphries & Smith, along with the British Museum shelf mark.

EDITIONS BY WALSH'S CONTEMPORARIES. *Figure 52 (upper left)*: Cluer opera score, 1724. *Figure 53 (upper right)*: Cooke keyboard music, 1739. *Figures 54 & 55 (bottom)*: John Johnson organ music, c.1745.

ENGLISH EDITIONS AROUND 1750. *Figure 56 (upper left)*: Walsh keyboard music, 1751. *Figure 57 (upper right)*: Kearsley song anthology, 1760. *Figure 58 (lower left)*: Johnson trio sonatas, c.1757. *Figure 59 (lower right)*: Bremner trio sonatas, 1763.

LATE 18TH-CENTURY ENGLISH EDITIONS. *Figure 60 (upper left)*: Longman trio sonatas, 1769. *Figure 61 (upper right)*: Thompson annual summer-gardens song anthology, 1788. *Figure 62 (lower left)*: John Bland trio sonatas, c.1782. *Figure 63 (lower right)*: Bland cantata score, 1785.

F. COPYRIGHT: For a detailed discussion of some of the problems see Alan Tyson, *The Authentic English Editions of Beethoven* (London 1963), Appendix I ("Entry at Stationers Hall"), pp. 131–43. Whatever the legal requirements, virtually no music was entered in the registers of Stationers Hall until about 1779.

The usual form of a copyright statement is "Entered at Stationers Hall"; but numerous musical works bearing these words were not, in fact, entered. Occasionally other phrases, such as "This Work is Copyright" or "This Work is Property," are found in music.

The archives of the Stationers Company at Stationers Hall, London, include several "Entry Books of Copies." In these books, manuscript entries were made for new publications, including music. For illustrations of these registers see Tyson, Plates XI–XII. The entries appear to have been transcribed from the title pages of the publications which were sent to Stationers Hall (Tyson, pp. 139–40). The registers for the period beginning 1 July 1842 are today preserved at the Public Record Office.

Many of the deposit copies are found today in the libraries that either receive such copies or once received them, as noted in M. below. At the British Museum, copyright deposit copies are identifiable by a blue stamp with the deposit date. Such dates were not noted on the copies until 1833: "In 1833 and 1834 the year, and sometimes the month, were noted; in 1835 and 1836 the month always appears, and from 1837 onward the exact day" (Neighbour & Tyson, p. 13).

G. ANNOUNCEMENTS: Throughout the period, daily newspapers such as *The Morning Post, The Public Advertiser, The World,* and others carried advertisements for new music. Many of the dates in the British Museum catalogues are based on these advertisements. New musical publications were regularly reviewed in *The Harmonicon* (1823–33), *The Quarterly Musical Magazine and Review* (1818–28), *The Musical Library* (1834–37), *The Musical World* (1836–91), and *The Musical Times* (1844–).

J. PAPER: "By an Act of Parliament of 1794 it proved financially advantageous to English publishers to mark their paper with a watermark date." See C.B. Oldman, "Watermark Dates in English Paper," *The Library*, IV, 25 (1944), pp. 70–71. "The Act from which the publishers benefited was abrogated in 1811, but such is the force of habit, that for many years after this watermark dates were still used in some paper"

LATE 18TH-CENTURY ENGLISH
EDITIONS IN OBLONG FOR-
MAT. *Figure 64 (top)*: Johnston
occasional song, 1769. *Figure 65
(right)*: Monzani cantata, 1791,
signed by the engraver. *Figure 66
(bottom)*: Birchall song collection
in quarto-size format, c.1790.

(Neighbour & Tyson, pp. 14–5). The watermark date is the date of the manufacture of the paper, not that of the publication of the music.

See also Jan LaRue, "British Music Paper, 1770–1820: Some Distinctive Characteristics," *Monthly Musical Record,* 87 (1957), 177–80.

K. CURRENCY: 1 pound (£) = 20 shillings; 1 shilling (s.) = 12 pence (d.) throughout the period of study. 1 guinea = 21 shillings. Kidson, p. 134, speculates that George Walker may have been "the first to institute the absurd practice of marking musical works at double the price intended to be asked."

L. IMPORTANT COLLECTIONS: The most extensive is **GB:Lbm.** There are also important holdings at **GB:Ob, GB:Cu, GB:E, GB:Ge, GB:M,** and **GB:Ckc.** In addition to the first four of these libraries, St. Andrews University and **EIR:Dtc** also have early copyright deposits. Among private collections, those of Gerald Coke in Bentley, the late Walter N.H. Harding in Chicago, and Alan Tyson in London are particularly important.

On the more general subject of British collectors see A. Hyatt King, *Some British Collectors of Music, c.1600–1960* (Cambridge 1963). The review by A.N.L. Munby in *The Book Collector,* 13 (1964), 242–6, contains additional information.

M. OTHER EVIDENCE: The dates in the *British Union-Catalogue of Early Music* (London 1957) are taken mostly from Squire's British Museum catalogue. They vary in reliability; many are approximations, rounded to the nearest likely year ending in a 0 or 5. More precise dates can often be found through newspaper advertisements.

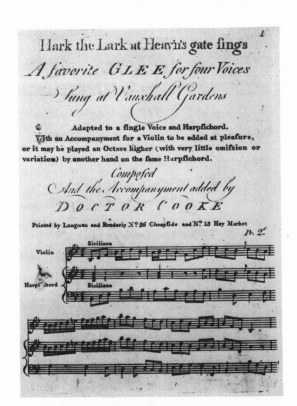

ENGLISH SONG SHEETS AND KEYBOARD MUSIC AROUND 1800. *Figure 67 (upper left):* Longman & Broderip. *Figure 68 (upper right):* Boag. *Figure 69 (lower left):* John Bland. *Figure 70 (lower right):* Broderip & Wilkinson.

EARLY 19TH-CENTURY ENGLISH EDITIONS. *Figure 71 (upper left):* Chappell glee book, 1808. *Figure 72 (upper right):* Walker descriptive piano piece, c.1814. *Figure 73 (lower left):* Boosey operatic aria, c.1815. *Figure 74 (lower right):* Oratorio score, 1817.

ENGLISH EDITIONS AFTER THE REGENCY. *Figure 75 (upper left)*: Royal Harmonic Institution descriptive piano piece, c.1823. *Figure 76 (upper right)*: Lonsdale art song, 1840. *Figure 77 (lower left)*: Goulding, d'Almaine, Potter, & Co. violin sonata, c.1822. *Figure 78 (lower right)*: Chappell operatic aria, 1836.

ENGLISH EDITIONS AFTER 1850. *Figure 79 (top)*: Two facing pages from an Addison & Hollier anthem collection, 1853, with double pagination. *Figure 80 (lower left)*: Ashdown & Parry song sheet, c.1860. *Figure 81 (lower right)*: Illustrated song sheet, c.1855, with the composer's control signature near the first musical system (the signature at the top is that of an owner). On the last two of these (as on Figures 235–7) the squared open letters, distinctive to this period, can be seen.

II. *The Netherlands*

ALFONS ANNEGARN, MARIE H. CHARBON,
CARI JOHANSSON, & PAUL VAN REIJEN

A. SUMMARIES: The only survey is J.P. Heije, "Muziekdrukkers en uitgevers," *Bouwsteenen, Jaarboeken der Vereeniging voor Noord-Nederlands Muziekgeschiedenis*, 1 (1869–72), 79–91; 2 (1872–4), 180–3; 3 (1874–81), 111–3.

B. DIRECTORIES: Extensive and useful data are to be found in the following:

A.M. Ledeboer, *De boekdrukkers, boekverkoopers en uitgevers in Noord-Nederland sedert de uitvinding van de boekdrukkunst tot den aanvang der negentiende eeuw* (Deventer 1872); *Alfabetische lijst* (Utrecht 1876); *Chronologisch register* (Utrecht 1876–7).

M.M. Kleerkoper & W.P. van Stockum, Jr., *De boekhandel te Amsterdam voornamelijk in de 17e eeuw* ('s-Gravenhage 1914–6).

E.F. Kossmann, "Eenige Haagsche muziekuitgevers der negentiende eeuw," *Die Haghe Jaarboek* (1928–9), 227–72.

——, *De boekhandel te 's-Gravenhage tot het eind van de 18de eeuw* ('s-Gravenhage 1937).

C. IMPORTANT NAMES:

Roger & LeCène, in Amsterdam, c.1695–1743. See François Lesure, *Bibliographie des Éditions musicales publiées par Estienne Roger et Michel-Charles LeCène* (Paris 1969); also Klaus Hortschansky, "Selbstverständnis und Verantwortung des Musikverlegers," *Neue Zeitschrift für Musik*, 131 (1970), 295–300. See Figure 82.

Pierre **Mortier**, in Amsterdam, founded c.1709. See François Lesure, "E. Roger et Pierre Mortier: Un épisode de la guerre des contrefaçons," *Revue de musicologie*, 38 (1956), 35–48.

Pietro **Locatelli**, in Amsterdam, 1721–1762, as publisher of his own op.1–9. See Arend Koole, *Leven en werken van Pietro Locatelli da Bergamo, 1695–1764* (Amsterdam 1949), pp. 10–16, 48ff., 130; also Albert Dunning & A. Koole, "Locatelli; Nieuwe bijdragen tot de kennis van zijn leven en werken," *Tijdschrift van de Vereniging voor Nederlandse Muziekgeschiedenis*, 20 (1964–5), 52–96.

G.H. **Witvogel**, in Amsterdam, 1731–1744. See Albert Dunning, *De muziekuitgever Gerhard Fredrik Witvogel et zijn fonds* (Utrecht 1966).

Johannes **Cóvens**, in Amsterdam, also other members of his family and their associates, c.1730–c.1850.

S. **Markordt**, in Amsterdam, fl.c.1780. See Figure 83.

Joseph **Schmitt**, in Amsterdam, and his successor, Vincent Springer, 1772/3–1798. See Albert Dunning, *Joseph Schmitt* (Amsterdam 1962), pp. 30–37.

The **Hummel** family, in Amsterdam, The Hague, and Berlin: Johann Julius Hummel and his successors in Amsterdam, 1754–1822, also in Berlin beginning in 1774. Burchard Hummel and his successors in The Hague, 1755–1801?, also in Amsterdam beginning in 1782. Generally identified as "B. Hummel et fils," or "B. Hummel en Zoon" beginning in 1781. The definitive study of the firm is Cari Johansson, *J.J. & B. Hummel, Music-Publishing and Thematic Catalogues* (Stockholm 1972). See Figures 84–5.

In The Hague, F.J. **Weygandt**, father and son, 1805–1895. See Figures 87–8.

In Rotterdam, Ludwig **Plattner**, 1810–c.1840. A study of this firm by Mrs. J.C. Mazure is to be issued in the *Tijdschrift van de Vereniging voor Nederlandse Muziekgeschiedenis*. See Figure 86.

D. PLATE NUMBERS:

N. Barth (Rotterdam, Noort Blaak; late 18th and early 19th century):

Numbers to around 200, undated, before 1800

F. Beuster (The Hague):

1 : 1836

AMSTERDAM EDITIONS OF THE 18TH CENTURY. *Figure 82 (upper left):* Le Cène instrumental parts, c.1733. *Figure 83 (upper right):* Markordt chamber music, c.1790. *Figures 84 & 85 (bottom):* Hummel instrumental editions, c.1775.

Correspondence Musicale (The Hague, 19th century):

Numbers to above 3000, undated

Cóvens (Amsterdam, Vijgendam; successors to Weygandt):

94, 95 : 1752, continuing Weygandt series
2 : 1756, Cóvens, Jr.

F.L. Dony (The Hague, Weenestraat 174, 1825–1829; Dony & Comp., Spuistraat 37 thereafter; also in Leyden, 1837–1841):

190 : 1851

L. & A.J. Hagenaar (Amsterdam, Stilsteeg 13; early 19th century):

Fewer than 25 numbers, undated

J.H. Henning (Amsterdam, Rokin; c.1790– before 1829):

130 : 1799

Hummel. From the plate number lists in Johansson, *Hummel*, 1, 80–117, the assignments below would appear to be appropriate.

				: date
? 11				: 1756
13 14				: 1757
15 18				: 1758
18 21				: 1759
?				
	95 99			: 1766
	82 92			: 1767
	70 83	?		: 1768
?				
149 150				: 1768/9
151 152				: 1769
	108 141			: 1770
201 204	100 109			: 1771
211 230				: 1772
236 255				
300 309				: 1773
310 329				: 1774
341 349	2 7			: 1775
	7 11			
350 367	46 50			: 1776
368 379	144 153			: 1777
380 392	152 163			: 1778
393 408	161 178			: 1779
406 416	179 193			: 1780
416 427	494 522			: 1781
429 433	520 544			: 1782
436 437	546 553			: 1783
442 457	557 583			: 1784
457 476	584 600			: 1785
479 494	602 612			: 1786

			: date
702 710	615 634		: 1787
714 727	635 644		: 1788
733 738	649 657		: 1789
739 745	658 674		: 1790
748 761	676 698		: 1791
762 773	800 811		: 1792
774 799	815 834	} : 1793
901 904			
905 909	836 842		: 1794
918 932	844 858		: 1795
942 958	865 882		: 1796
962 1004	885 895		: 1797
1009 1014	1104 1110		: 1798
1023 1030	1114 1137		: 1799
1033 1042	1139 1157		: 1800
1046 1058	1161 1168		: 1801
1060 1073	1169 1183		: 1802
1075 1085	1184 1202		: 1803
1088 1099	1203 1214		: 1804
1304 1320	1239 1253		: 1805
1340 1409			: inter 1806/8
1418			: 1809?
1485			: 1813/4
1488 1493			: 1814
1518 1583			: inter 1814/9
1585 1604			: inter 1820?/2

For a thorough discussion of Hummel plate numbers, however, see
Johansson, v.1, pp. 10–11. Of course, Johansson's dates obviate the use of
plate numbers for dating purposes, making the above chart useful mainly
as a proposed overview of the system, its sequence based on assigned
"blocks" of numbers.

C.G.A. Lotter & Comp. (The Hague, before 1838):

Fewer than 25 numbers, undated

W.C. Nolting (Amsterdam, Kalverstraat 80; c.1785– after 1830):

121	: 1816
279	: 1819
284	: 1820
412	: 1831
419	: 1833

Name forms are as follows: c.1785–c.1804: W.C. Nolting; c.1804–c.1806:
Veuve W.C. Nolting; c.1806–c.1816: Veuve W.C. Nolting et fils; after c.1816:
J.B. Nolting.

Arnold Olofsen (Amsterdam, c.1750):

1–3 for three editions of Mahaut's music

Ludwig Plattner (Rotterdam):

635	: 1820
835	: 1830
871	: 1833

Numbers extend to above 1000

Roger & LeCène (Amsterdam). See Deutsch, pp. 19–21, and especially
Lesure's *Bibliographie* of the firm. Plate numbers to 411 are within the
scope of the 1716 catalogue, and are cited by Lesure on pp. 57–87.
Numbers 412–594 are summarized in the "Tableau des Cotages" four
pages later.

Th.J. Roothan & Cie. (Amsterdam):

	124	: 1857
	140	: 1859
	147	: 1860
160	162	: 1861
168	187	: 1862

Other numbers extend as high as 340 (1871). Mr. Van Reijen has a list of them, also of numbers of other members of the Roothan family, A. in Amsterdam, L. in Utrecht.

L.W. Roumen (Amsterdam Kalverstraat 92):

	221	: 1831	255	266	: 1834
234	243	: 1832		269	: 1835
	250	: 1833		281	: 1838
				283	: 1839

H.C. Steup (Amsterdam, Spui, c.1780–c.1801, Kalverstraat 203, c.1801–1830):

	121	: 1816
143	174	: 1819
180	196	: 1820
	225	: after 1821

Theune & Comp. (Amsterdam, Kalverstraat 80):

	19	: 1830	65–71, 91	: 1837
21	22	: 1831	80	: 1838
27	34	: 1832	118	: 1839
	38	: 1833	160	: 1840
	39	: 1834	272	: 1841
44	45	: 1835	618	: 1852
53	58	: 1836	647	: 1854

Aris Tolk (Edam, end of the 18th century):

Only a few numbers are known, all undated

J. Vermazzen (Amsterdam, Nes 79):

112 : 1826

W.C. de Vletter (Rotterdam, succeeded in 1862 by Weygandt):

311 : 1854

F.J. Weygandt (The Hague & Amsterdam, 1805–1895):

1000	: 1837	1288–89	: 1847
1023	: 1839	1625	: 1859
1056	: 1840	1911	: 1865
1268–73	: 1846	1915	: 1867

The history of the firm is characterized by frequent address changes:

1805–1814: "Au Parnasse," Korte Poten 406, The Hague
1814–1822: Spuistraat 115, The Hague

1822–1825: Kalverstraat 229, Amsterdam, with two shops in The Hague, at Spuistraat 115 and at Korte Poten 379, the latter managed by F.L. Dony

1825–1828: as above but with the Spuistraat shop closed, the Korte Poten shop now managed by F.L. Weygandt the son, and the imprint now reading, "F.J. Weygandt et fils"

1828–1833: as above, but with the Hague shop now located at Spuistraat 115, and the Korte Poten office not mentioned

1833–1837: F.J. Weygandt the father alone to the time of his death

1833–1835: "F.J. Weygandt fils" alone in the Hague at Korte Poten 379

1835–1839: as above, but the word "fils" is no longer mentioned

1839–1858: F.J. Weygandt et Beuster, Nieuwstraat 169, The Hague

1859–1895: F.J. Weygand et Comp., often with the name of the manager added, i.e., L.J. Febèbre, 1863–1875; and J. Muzerie, 1875–1895

G.J. Witvogel (Amsterdam, Warmoesgracht, 1731–1744): see the monograph by Dunning, pp. 38–54.

E. CATALOGUES: Those issued by Roger are either reproduced or transcribed in Lesure. Those by Hummel are reproduced in facsimile and discussed in Johansson. Among those lost is one for Schmitt from 1793: see Dunning, p. 35.

F. COPYRIGHT: According to librarians at the University of Leyden, privileges were granted as early as the 16th century. As of 1700, publishers were required to submit a copy, which was held at the university library in Leyden. During the 18th century, however, these copies were deemed worthless and were sold. Unfortunately, the registration records have also been lost.

G. ANNOUNCEMENTS: Beginning around 1650, announcements were printed in the newspapers, which were published one or more times a week, such as the *Amsterdamse Courant, Haarlemsche Courant,* or *'s-Gravenhaagsche Courant.*

K. CURRENCY: 1 florin (guilder) = 20 stuivers. This was used throughout the period of study. Hummel editions distributed through Berlin frequently have a price in Reichsthalers. During the time of the so-called Batavian Republic, 1795–1806, French currencies were used.

L. IMPORTANT COLLECTIONS: The largest are N:At, N:AN, N:DHgm, N:DHk, N:DHa, N:Lu, N:Uim, N:Usg. Other valuable collections are at N:DHmw, N:H, N:R, and N:Uu.

19TH-CENTURY EDITIONS FROM THE LOW COUNTRIES. *Figure 86 (upper left)*: Plattner decorative title-page design (Rotterdam c.1810). *Figure 87 (upper right)*: Weygandt piano music (The Hague c.1820). *Figure 88 (lower left)*: Weygandt piano music (c.1850). *Figure 89 (lower right)*: Messemaeckers piano music (Brussels c.1840).

III. *Belgium*

BERNARD HUYS

A. SUMMARIES: Alphonse Goovaerts, *Histoire et bibliographie de la typographie musicale dans les Pays-Bas* (Antwerp 1880) is concerned mostly with the period before 1700, but is also useful as a point of departure for later periods.

C. IMPORTANT NAMES: In the 19th century, Henri **Messemaeckers**, **Van Ypen & Pris**, and **Mechtler**, all in Brussels, and Benoit **Andrez** in Liège. See Figure 89.

L. IMPORTANT COLLECTIONS: **B:Bc** is by far the strongest, **B:Br** also has important material.

EARLY FRENCH ENGRAVINGS.
Figure 90 (top): Chédeville contradances, c.1735. *Figure 91 (right)*: Rameau opera, 1739. *Figure 92 (bottom)*: La Chevardière edition of a Philidor opera, 1759.

IV. *France*

FRANÇOIS LESURE

B. DIRECTORIES: The basic work is Cecil Hopkinson, *A Dictionary of Parisian Music Publishers, 1700–1950* (London 1954), based largely on the early directories. Some lesser 19th-century publishers are omitted. A revised edition is now being prepared.

C. IMPORTANT NAMES. Among many in Paris, the following are particularly important:

H. **Foucault**, 1702–1721.

Charles-Nicolas **Le Clerc**, 1736–1774, music publisher of the family of music dealers which was active as early as 1713, often in conjunction with the dealer François **Boivin**, 1722–1734? See Sylviette Milliot, "Un couple de marchands de musique au XVIIIe siècle: Les Boivin," *Revue de musicologie*, 54 (1968), 105–13. See Figures 93, 95.

Christophe **Le Menu**, 1742–1784; Mme Le Menu, 1775–1790, with Mme **Boyer**, 1776?–1783; M. Boyer, 1783–1796, alone & with Mme Le Menu. See Johansson (cited in E. below), pp. 104–33. See Figures 96, 98.

Bayard, 1754–1762.

Louis Balthasar de la **Chevardière**, 1758–1785? Johansson, pp. 61–84. See Figure 92.

Antoine **Huberty**, c.1757–c.1778, later in Vienna. Johansson, pp. 40–51; see also the study of his Viennese career by Weinmann.

Jean Baptiste **Venier**, 1760–1783. Johansson, pp. 155–69.

Antoine **Bailleux**, c.1761?–1795. Johansson, pp. 9–20. See Figure 3.

Bureau d'Abonnement Musicale, 1765–1783. Johansson, pp. 21–39.

Jacques Georges **Cousineau**, and his son Pierre Joseph, 1767–1823.

Simon **Le Duc**, c.1768–1777, his brother Pierre Le Duc, 1775–1780,

153

and their heirs, among them Alphonse, who reorganized the firm in 1841. Johansson, pp. 85–103. See Figure 101.

Jean Georges **Sieber**, 1771–1814, his widow to 1822, and his son, Georges Julien, working independently, c.1798–1834. Johansson, pp. 134–54. See Anik Devries, "Les éditions musicales Sieber," *Revue de musicologie*, 55 (1969), 20–46. See Figure 99.

Jean Henry **Naderman** and his heirs, 1777–1835.

J.J. **Imbault**, c.1785–1814. Johansson, pp. 52–60. See Paule Guiomar, "J.J. Imbault," *Fontes artis musicae*, 13 (1966), 43–6. See Figures 103, 104, 106.

The **Gaveaux** family, 1793–1832.

The **Lemoine** family, founded 1793. See Figure 111.

Magasin de musique . . ., 1794–1825.

Jouve, c.1795–1835.

Ignace Joseph **Pleyel**, 1795–1834. See Rita Benton, "A la recherche de Pleyel perdu," *Fontes artis musicae,* 17 (1970), 9–15, by way of anticipating her major study of the man and his works. See Figure 100.

Mlles. **Erard**, 1798–1840.

J.J. **Momigny**, 1800–1828. See Albert Palm, "J.J. de Momigny als Verleger," *Fontes artis musicae*, 10 (1963), 42–59. (Hopkinson, p. 36).

The **Choron** family, 1805–1852.

Charles Simon **Richault** & heirs, 1805–1893. See Figures 115, 118.

Antonio Francesco Gaetano **Pacini**, 1806–1846. See Figures 105, 107.

R. **Carli** et Cie., 1809–1829.

Janet et Cotelle, 1810–1838; A. Cotelle alone until his death in 1858. The firm continued under his name until 1892. See Figure 102.

Louis Armand Dauphin **Boieldieu**, 1811–1824.

Jacques Josfa **Frey**, 1811–1840. See Figure 108.

A. **Meissonnier** Ainé, 1812–1839, in partnership with J.L. **Heugel**,

FRENCH "CLASSICAL" EDITIONS. *Figure 93 (upper left):* Boivin & Le Clerc dances, c.1735. *Figure 94 (upper right):* Dramatic score, 1749. *Figure 95 (lower left):* Le Clerc opera score, c.1765. *Figure 96 (lower left):* Boyer keyboard music, c.1787.

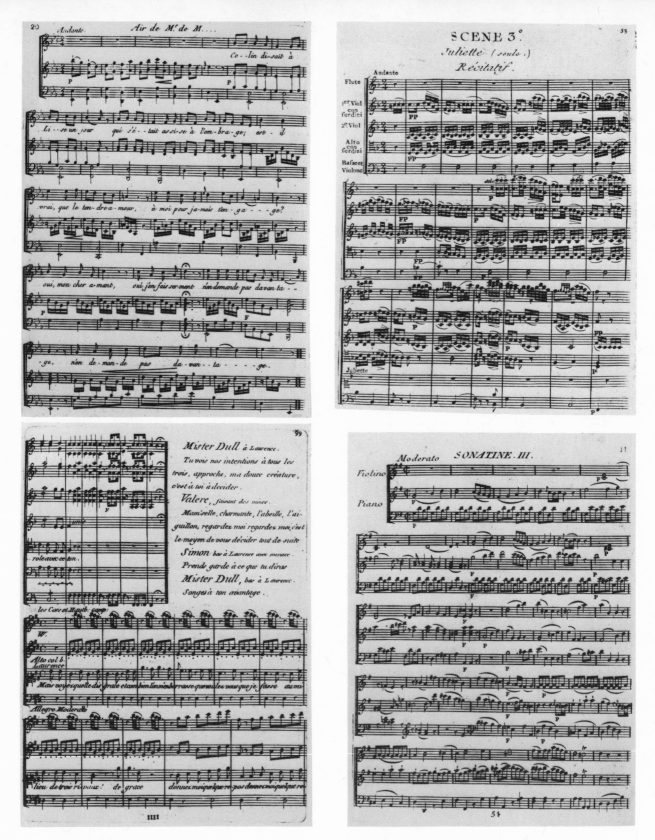

LATE 18TH-CENTURY FRENCH EDITIONS. *Figure 97 (upper left):* Song collection, c.1785. *Figure 98 (upper right):* Boyer opera score, 1793. *Figure 99 (lower left):* Sieber opera score, c.1790. *Figure 100 (lower right):* Pleyel keyboard music, c.1797.

EARLY 19TH-CENTURY FRENCH EDITIONS OF INSTRUMENTAL MUSIC. *Figure 101 (upper left):* Le Duc trio sonatas. *Figure 102 (upper right):* Janet & Cotelle piano music. *Figure 103 (lower left):* Imbault piano music. *Figure 104 (lower right):* Imbault trio sonatas.

1839–1842, thereafter Heugel alone; J. Meissonnier Jeune, and his heirs, 1828?–1860.

Collinet Père, 1813–1855.

Jacques Hippolyte Aristide **Farrenc**, 1819–1844.

Maurice Adolphe **Schlesinger**, son of the Berlin publisher, 1821–1846. See Deutsch, *Musikverlagsnummern*, p. 22. See Figures 109, 113.

J.A. **Aulagnier**, 1822–1867.

E. **Troupenas**, 1825–1850. See Figures 110, 114, 116.

Launer, 1828–1854.

Schonenberger, 1830–1875. See Figure 112.

Canaux, 1839–1869, after 1856 identified as Régnier-Canaux.

Leon **Escudier**, as the **Bureau Central** de la Musique, 1841–1882.

Gemmy **Brandus**, 1846–1887, after 1854 in partnership with S. **Dufour**. See Figures 4, 117.

The major publishers in Lyon:

Antoine **De Bretonne**, 1735–1757, and his successors, Les Frères **Le Goux**, 1758–1769.

Castaud, 1765–1784, and his successor, **Garnier**, 1801–1803.

Guéra, 1777–1782.

For further information, see Hopkinson.

D. PLATE NUMBERS: The *Fontes artis musicae* list is useful partly as a reminder of how much work needs to be done. Certain publishers, among them Heugel, have preserved in their archives the records of their plate numbers. Several studies which include information on French plate numbers are cited in C. above. The file of Richault numbers in the New York Public Library is said to be especially valuable.

E. CATALOGUES: Cari Johansson, *French Music Publishers' Catalogues of the Second Half of the Eighteenth Century* (Stockholm 1955)

FRENCH EDITIONS DURING THE SECOND REPUBLIC. *Figure 105 (upper left)*: Pacini piano music. *Figure 106 (upper right)*: Imbault piano music; cf. Figures 6–11, which show the London edition of this same work. *Figure 107 (lower left)*: Pacini chamber music. *Figure 108 (lower right)*: Frey oratorio score.

covers nine of the most important firms (see C. above). In addition, other bibliographical sources are discussed, and 146 facsimile reproductions are included. See also her summary, "Publishers' Addresses as a Guide to the Dating of French Printed Music of the Second Half of the Eighteenth Century," *Fontes artis musicae*, 1 (1954), 14–19.

Additional catalogues located in the Library of Congress, Washington, are cited by D.W. Krummel in *Fontes artis musicae*, 7 (1960), 61–4.

Several more facsimiles are reproduced in Barry Brook, *La Symphonie française* (Paris 1962). A number of 19th-century catalogues exist but have not been collected.

F. COPYRIGHT AND LEGAL DEPOSIT: The various programs fall into three categories.

1. Privileges, 1654–1789. Registration books for the royal privileges are in the Bibliothèque Nationale, Paris (Mss. franç. 16754, 21944-71). Extracts were published in Michel Brenet, "La Librairie musicale en France de 1653 à 1790 d'après les registres de privilèges," *SIMG*, 8 (1906–7), 401–66. Other extracts not covered by Brenet are described (less precisely) in Georges Cucuel, "Quelques documents sur la librairie musicale au XVIIIe siècle," *ibid.*, 13 (1911–12), 385–92.

2. Dépôt legal, since 1811. The Archives Nationales, Paris, has the registration records for both Parisian publications, 1811–1828 and 1842–1912 (Série F 18-VIII), and provincial publications, 1849–1885, with some gaps (Série F 18-XII). Registration records after 1912 are in the Bibliothèque Nationale. Depository copies received in the Bibliothèque Nationale between 1839 and c.1880 bear a red stamp with the date of deposit. The call numbers also usually indicate that these are depository copies.

3. Timbre fiscal, 1797–1806. On 30 October 1797 a duty was imposed on "la musique 'en feuilles,'" that is, separate songs and periodical series, e.g., "sheet music." Because the stamps used for the duty were often changed, their appearance is useful in dating for the period extending from the enactment up to the year 1806, not only for French publications but also for those issued in territories under French occupation. The stamps are studied and reproduced in Elisabeth Lebeau, "Le timbre fiscal de la musique en feuilles de 1797 à 1840," *Revue de musicologie*, 27 (1945), 20–8.

FRENCH EDITIONS OF THE GRAND OPERA PERIOD. *Figure 109 (upper left):* Schlesinger c.1831. *Figure 110 (upper right):* Troupenas, c.1839. *Figure 111 (lower left):* Lemoine c.1855. *Figure 112 (lower right):* Schonenberger, c. 1835.

G. ANNOUNCEMENTS: In the 18th century, new music was advertized in the following important journals: *Mercure de France, Journal de Paris, Gazette de Paris*, and *Annonces, affiches et avis divers.* ... The "Fichier Peyrot" is now in the Bibliothèque Nationale, and has been used often by scholars, particularly for many *MGG* articles. A new abstract is being made, along systematic lines, in the Département de la Musique. Among many important studies which have cited these announcements are Johansson, Brook, also H. Gougelot, *La romance française sous la Révolution et l'Empire* (Melun 1938), and L. de la Laurencie, *L'école française de violon, de Lully à Viotti* (Paris 1922–4).

Equally important is the *Journal de la librairie et des arts*, issued since 1782, and still in existence in modified form as the *Bibliographie de la France*. Since 1810 a specific rubric has been assigned to music, and since 1946 the music section has appeared as a special supplement. In addition, useful information on French music publishers may be found in Frits Noske, *La Mélodie française de Berlioz à Duparc* (Paris 1954; Engl. translation with added appendices by Rita Benton, New York 1970), and in the catalogues of Gluck (1959, 1967), Berlioz (1951), and Verdi (1973) by Cecil Hopkinson and of Boccherini (1969) by Yves Gérard.

K. CURRENCY: Before 1794:

> 1 livre = 20 sols
> 1 sol = 4 liards = 12 deniers

After 1794:

> 1 franc = 10 decimes = 100 centimes

L. IMPORTANT COLLECTIONS: F:Pn, with F:Pc and F:Po, is preeminent. The distinguished personal collections of Geneviève Thibault, André Meyer, Germaine de Rothschild, and Marc Pincherle are likewise important.

FRENCH EDITIONS AROUND 1850. *Figure 113 (top):* Schlesinger opera vocal score, 1840, in "Parisian" format with the plate number in the bottom inner margin. *Figure 114 (lower left):* Troupenas edition of Labarre's *Album*, 1842. *Figure 115 (lower right):* Richault chamber music of the 1840s.

FRENCH OPERA VOCAL SCORES AROUND 1850. *Figure 116 (top):* Troupenas score with the plate number in the typical "Parisian" format location. *Figure 117 (lower left):* Brandus score. *Figure 118 (lower right):* Richault score.

V. Spain

HERMANN & GERDA BARON

There are two major publishers who absorbed a number of the smaller firms: **Boileau** in Barcelona and the **Union Musical Española** in Madrid. The latter firm made a "take-over bid" in 1900, which must be unique in the history of music publishing: some two dozen-odd firms, with all their stock as well as their archives, were absorbed at one time. The names of these publishers (some of whom are obviously related) are:

Luis E. Dotesio

Antonio Romero y Andia   Casa Marzo
  (said to be the oldest   Almagro y Compañía
  music publisher)   Faustino Fuentes

Casa Romero   Rafael Guardia

Viuda de Romero   Casa Zozaya

Casimiro Martín   Emilio Zozaya y Guillen

Enrique Villegas   Eslava

Fuentes y Asenjo   Bonifacio San Martín Eslava

Lastra, Fuentes y Ansejo   Pablo Martín Larrony

Hijos de Vidal y Roger
Orfeo Tracio S.A.
Sociedad Editorial de Música
Ildefonso Alier
Juan Bautista Pujol
Vidal, Llimona y Boceta
Luís Tena
Juan Ayné
Sánchez Ferris
Salvat

In 1847, there began to appear, at irregular intervals, the *Boletín de la Propriedad Intelectual, poblicado por el Ministerio de Fomento* (later *por el Registro General de la Misma*), which contains dated entries for printed materials, including music. It should be stressed that the entries are reported to have been "selected"; on what basis is uncertain. Furthermore, Spanish law required the registration of every work which received even a single performance. Thus the dated entries may refer to works performed which remained in manuscript. Beginning with the years 1879–1881, the entries were cumulated in the triennial *Registro general de la Propriedad Intelectual*. The formidable task of extracting the published music from this work must obviously be undertaken.*

Among the major libraries, E:Mn and E:Bu have good holdings, but their catalogues do not attempt to supply dates.

---

*Special thanks are due to Señor Jaime Moll, general librarian at the Real Academia de la Lengua in Madrid, for calling attention to this work.

ITALIAN EDITIONS. *Figure 119 (top):* Venice: Zatta, c.1790. *Figure 120 (lower left):* Naples 1785. *Figure 121 (lower right):* Naples: Girard, c.1850.

VI. *Italy*

Information on the 19th Century
provided largely by PHILIP GOSSETT

B. DIRECTORIES: Claudio Sartori, *Dizionario degli editori musicali italiani* (Florence 1953) covers all periods of history. It lists major as well as many minor publishers, but includes little information about addresses and their relation to the publisher's career.

C. IMPORTANT NAMES: Between 1700 and 1810, music in Italy was circulated extensively in manuscript but was rarely printed. Over 100 printers and publishers from the 18th century are listed by Sartori. However, most of them issued treatises and service books, which were set in type, and dated, thus making these publications generally outside the scope of this study. Music specialists slowly emerged between 1770 and 1810, although their "editions" often consist of manuscript copies preceded by an engraved *passe-partout* title page. Among such firms were Innocente **Alessandri e Scattaglia** and Antonio **Zatta** in Venice, Luigi **Marescalchi** in Naples, and several members of the **Artaria** family in Milan. See Figures 119–20.

The firm of **Ricordi**, which has dominated Italian music publishing since its founding in 1808, is discussed in many sources, notably Claudio Sartori's *Casa Ricordi, 1808–1858* (Milan 1958). See Figures 122–3, 125–6.

Among other important firms of the 19th century are **Lucca** in Milan, **Girard** in Naples, and **Ratti, Cencetti, & Cie.** in Rome. See Figures 121, 124.

D. PLATE NUMBERS: Ricordi numbers are listed in Fuld, pp. 67–70; see also Thomas F. Heck, "Ricordi Plate Numbers, 1808–1857: A Chronological Survey," *Current Musicology*, 10 (1970), 117–23. These studies supersede the discussion in Cecil Hopkinson, *A Bibliography of the Musical and Literary Works of Hector Berlioz* (London 1951), and are supple-

167

mented by the lists in his *Bibliography of the Works of Guiseppe Verdi, 1813–1901,* v.1 (New York 1973), p. 93ff. See the Synopsis, I.C.2.c., Example 2.

Dated numbers and a summary discussion of plate numbers for publishers between 1808 and 1850 – notably Ricordi, Girard, and Ratti, Cencetti, & Cie., – appear in Philip Gossett, *The Operas of Rossini* (Princeton 1970), Appendix III. A fuller chronology of numbers for Ratti, Cencetti, & Cie. is as follows:

1	11	:	1821		323	:	1830
20	30	:	1822	379	380	:	1831
74	124	:	1823	438	448	:	1833
133	154	:	1824	561	568	:	1835
238	249	:	1828		599	:	1837

E. CATALOGUES: "A First List of Italian Music Publishers' Catalogues," prepared by Claudio Sartori, has been appended to his article, "The Bibliographer's Occupation," *Notes,* II, 26 (1970), 710–12. (To the list can be added a *Catalogo degli spartiti manoscritti d'opere teatrali d'ogni genere,* prepared by the Milan firm of Lucca in 1859: Theodore Thomas's copy is in the Newberry Library.)

Ricordi is also known to have included catalogues on wrappers of music which he published during 1819–1820. These *supplimenti* give detailed information about recent publications. Copies are known to exist in the Biblioteca Palatina (Sezione Musicale) in Parma.

F. COPYRIGHT: The state of Italian copyright laws is summarized in Fuld, pp. 21–3. It must be remembered that "Italy" was a political fiction before 1861, and thus each state must be considered separately.

G. ANNOUNCEMENTS: The most important source of these is Ricordi's *Gazzetta musicale di Milano,* beginning in 1842. Information on new musical editions from Naples can be found in the *Giornale delle due Sicilie.* Daily newspapers in various cities also carried occasional citations, but no attempt has been made to survey them systematically.

L. IMPORTANT COLLECTIONS: Major holdings are at I:Bc, I:Fc, I:Mc, I:Nc, and I:Rsc. A library of Verdi editions is being organized by

**TITLE DECORATION OF ITAL-
IAN OPERA ARIA EDITIONS.**
Figure 122 (top): Ricordi, 1832.
Figure 123 (right): Ricordi, 1856.
Figure 124 (bottom): Lucca, 1844.

the Istituto de Studi verdiana in Parma. The Ufficio Ricerca Fondi Musicali, maintained in Milan by Claudio Sartori, assisted by Mariangela Doná, has a massive union catalogue of Italian library holdings. Its offices (Via Clerici 5, Milano 20121) are maintained through the Biblioteca Nazionale Braidense.

M.   OTHER EVIDENCE:

1.   Composers. The relationship between the composer and his publisher deserves special attention. The works of Rossini have been studied by Philip Gossett; those of Verdi are being studied by Cecil Hopkinson.

2.   First Performances. Since so much of the music publishing in Italy during this period consisted of opera scores and excerpts, useful information can be gathered by comparing dates of opera premieres with the earliest publications of excerpts issued by publishers *in the city of its premiere.* Often the premiere and the publication date of the first excerpts were separated by no more than a week. (As the copyist was often the publisher as well, this is not surprising.) A publication date for operatic excerpts, particularly before 1850, can often be postulated from the first performance. In such cases, it is essential to know the habits of the publishers, composers, and opera houses involved, and to look for corroborating evidence.

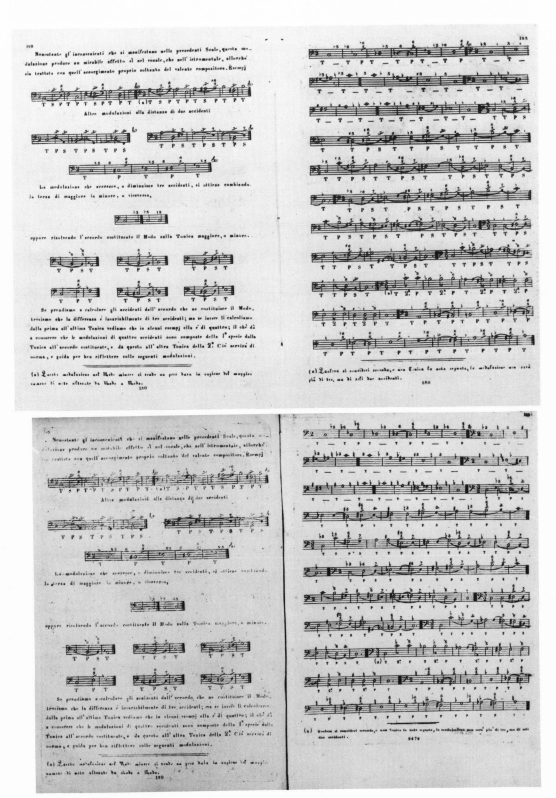

PLATE SUBSTITUTION IN A RICORDI EDITION. *Figure 125 (top)*: Original form, 1813. *Figure 126 (bottom)*: Later form, c.1836, with a different recto page which has a new plate number.

SWISS EDITIONS. *Figure 127 (upper left)*: Nägeli, 1800. *Figure 128 (upper right)*: Nägeli, 1801. *Figure 129 (lower left)*: Nägeli, c.1810. *Figure 130 (lower right)*: Rieter-Biedermann, c.1850.

VII. *Switzerland*

ROBERT WYLER & HANS-RUDOLF DÜRRENMATT

C. IMPORTANT NAMES:

Hans-Georg **Nägeli**, in Zürich, founded 1791. See Hermann Josef Schattner, *Volksbildung durch Musikerziehung: Leben und Wirken Hans Georg Nägelis* (Osterbach-Kaiserslautern 1961), pp. 238–93: "Der Verlag H.G. Nägeli"; also Georg Walter, *Die Schicksale des Autographs der h-moll-Messe von J.S. Bach; ein Beitrag zur zürcherischen Musikverlagsgeschichte* (Zürich 1965; 149. Neujahrsblatt der Allgemeinen Musikgesellschaft Zürich), also other writings mentioned in Hans-Martin Plesske's bibliography (cited in VIII.A. below), items 412–21. See Figures 127–9.

Jakob Melchior **Rieter-Biedermann**, in Winterthur, 1849–1862, later in Leipzig. References are cited in Plesske, items 555–60. See Figure 130.

D. PLATE NUMBERS:
An index, covering the German-speaking parts of Switzerland, is now being established by Dr. Dürrenmatt at the Musikwissenschaftliches Seminar der Universität Bern, Längassstrasse 7).

K. CURRENCY:
There is no uniform monetary system in Switzerland during this period.

L. IMPORTANT COLLECTIONS:
CH:Bu, CH:BEl, CH:Gu, CH:Zz.

BREITKOPF EDITIONS, ILLUS-
TRATING THE THREE DIFFER-
ENT PRINTING PROCESSES. *Fig-
ure 131 (top)*: Lithographed, c.1810.
Figure 132 (right): Type-set, 1813.
Figure 133 (bottom): Engraved,
1826.

VIII. *Germany*

LIESBETH WEINHOLD

A. SUMMARIES AND BIBLIOGRAPHIES: Both German music publishing and the literature on German music publishing have been prolific. There is no one single standard survey of the whole field, however. The following works are particularly useful for information.

A comprehensive general bibliography of the entire field is found in Hans-Martin Plesske, "Bibliographie des Schrifttums zur Geschichte deutscher und österreichischer Musikverlage," *Beiträge zur Geschichte des Buchwesens*, 3 (1968), 135–222.

Richard Schaal's article, "Musikverlag und Musikhandel," *MGG*, v.9 (1967), c. 1178–91, gives a useful general survey and mentions important names.

Useful background information may be found in Max Schumann, *Zur Geschichte des deutschen Musikalienhandels seit der Gründung des Vereins der Deutschen Musikalienhändler, 1829–1929* (Leipzig 1929).

The massive Hofmeister *Handbuch der musikalischen Literatur* lists new German publications, as well as many foreign ones. (See the discussion of this set below.)

Music publishers are also frequently discussed in books on publishing in general, such as Friedrich Kapp & Johann Goldfriedrich, *Geschichte des deutschen Buchhandels* (Leipzig 1886–1923); Rudolf Schmidt, *Deutsche Buchhändler, Deutsch Buchdrucker . . .* (Berlin 1902–1908); K. Löffler, *et al.*, *Lexikon des gesamten Buchwesens* (Leipzig 1935–1937); Joachim Kirchner, *Lexikon des Buchwesens* (Stuttgart 1952–1956); and the *Lexikon der deutschen Verlage* (Leipzig 1929).

Information on all aspects of the history of German music publishing is being collected through the Arbeitsgemeinschaft für Geschichte der deutschen Musikpublikation. See the notice by F.W. Riedel in *Die Musikforschung*, 18 (1965), 416–20.

B. DIRECTORIES: Ernst Challier, *Verlags-Nachweis im Musikalienhandel* (Giessen 1908–13) is most specifically concerned with firms that have gone out of existence. A similar work covering all kinds of publishers is Albert Erlecke, *Die Besitz- und Firmenänderungen im deutschen Verlags-, Buch-, Kunst-, Musikalien-, und Landkartenhandel, 1750–1885* (Leipzig 1886).

175

C. IMPORTANT NAMES: (For further references see Plesske as noted. Full citations cover the most important recent writings, many of which are the result of the efforts of members of the Arbeitsgemeinschaft für Geschichte der Musikpublikation.)

Bernhard Christoph Breitkopf and successors, i.e., notably Johann Gottlob Immanuel Breitkopf, and finally **Breitkopf & Härtel**, in Leipzig, founded 1719. Among the writings for the 150th anniversary of the firm, see Hellmuth von Hase, *Breitkopf & Härtel, Gedenkschrift und Arbeitsbericht, 3: 1918–1968* (Wiesbaden 1968); Irene Hempel, *Pasticcio auf das 250jährige Bestehen des Verlages Breitkopf & Härtel* (Leipzig 1968); Rudolf Elvers, *Breitkopf & Härtel, 1719–1969; Ein historischer Überblick* zum *Jubiläum (Wiesbaden 1968); Musikalien herausgegeben anlässlich des 250jährigen Bestehens des Musikverlags Breitkopf & Härtel* (Leipzig 1969); Plesske 206–79. See Figures 12–13, 131–6.

Johann Jakob **Lotter** and his successors, in Augsburg, 1719–c.1844. Plesske 481–4.

Balthasar **Schmid** and his successors, in Nuremberg, 1725–c.1786. See Horst Heussner, "Nürnberger Musikverlag und Musikhandel im 18. Jahrhunderts," in *Musik und Verlag* (Vötterle Festschrift; Kassel 1968), pp. 319–41; Plesske 567.

Johann Ulrich **Haffner**, in Nuremberg, 1740–1770. Plesske 338–9.

Bernhard **Schott** and his successors, in Mainz, founded 1770. See Hans Schneider, "Zur Datierung der Musikdrucke des Verlages B. Schott's Söhne," *Aus dem Antiquariat* (supplement to the Frankfurt *Börsenblatt für den deutschen Buchhandel*), 27 (1971), A32–6; Plesske 568–96. See Figures 148–9.

Johann Julius **Hummel**, in Berlin, 1770–c.1822, as a branch of the Dutch firm discussed in II. above.

Johann Michael **Götz**, in Mannheim, later in Worms, Munich, and Düsseldorf, 1773–1802? Plesske 336–7. See Figure 137.

Nicolaus **Haueisen**, in Frankfurt am Main, 1771–1789. See Wolfgang Matthäus, "Der Musikverlag von Wolfgang Nicolaus Haueisen zu Frankfurt am Main, 1771–1789," *Die Musikforschung*, 22 (1969), 421–42.

176   Johann **André** and his successors, in Offenbach am Main, founded

BREITKOPF AND GÖTZ EDITIONS. *Figure 134 (upper left)*: Breitkopf lithographed piano music, c.1816. *Figure 135 (upper right)*: Breitkopf engraved piano music, 1837. *Figure 136 (lower left)*: Breitkopf engraved chamber music, 1850. *Figure 137 (lower right)*: Götz chamber music, c.1785, with distinctive punches.

EARLY SIMROCK EDITIONS.
Figure 138 (top): c.1794. *Figure 138 (top):* c.1794. *Figure 139 (right):* c.1803. *Figure 140 (bottom):* c.1818.

LATER SIMROCK EDITIONS. *Figure 141 (right):* c.1839. *Figure 142 (lower left):* 1851. *Figure 143 (lower right):* c.1850.

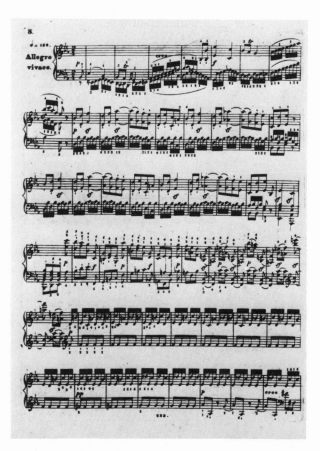

1774. A history of the family and the firm by Klaus Hortschansky, and a bibliography by the late Wolfgang Matthäus, are being published for the 200th anniversary of the firm. Plesske 116–27. See Figures 144–6.

Heinrich Philipp **Bossler**, in Speyer, later in Darmstadt and in Gohlis near Leipzig, 1781–1828. Plesske 179; Hans Schneider has also been studying this publisher.

F.E.C. **Leuckart**, in Breslau, 1782–1870. Plesske 446–54.

Johann Karl Friedrich **Rellstab**, in Berlin, 1782–1806. Plesske 541–2.

Macario **Falter**, in Munich, 1787–1888. See Hans Schmid, "Falter & Sohn; Ein Münchner Musikverlag des 19. Jahrhunderts," *Mitteilungsblatt der Gesellschaft für Bayerische Musikgeschichte*, 6 (1973), 108–16; Liesbeth Weinhold has also been studying this firm. See Figure 147.

Nikolaus **Simrock**, in Bonn, c.1790–1870. Plesske 617–32. See Figures 138–43.

G. **Gombart** & Co., in Augsburg, 1795–c.1844. (See Synopsis, VI.C.1. Note)

Johann August **Böhme**, in Hamburg, 1794–1885; also as Günther & Böhme, c.1792–1799. See Figure 157.

Musikalisches Magazin **auf der Höhe** (Johann Peter **Spehr**), in Braunschweig, c.1794–1844.

Franz Anton **Hoffmeister** (with two f's, and from Vienna), with Ambrosius **Kühnel**, in Leipzig, 1800–1805; Kühnel alone, 1805–1814; succeeded by C.F. **Peters**, since 1814. See Heinrich Lindlar, *C.F. Peters Musikverlag: Zeittafeln zur Verlagsgeschichte, 1800–1867–1967* (Frankfurt 1967); Plesske 515–33. See Figures 150–2, 155–6.

Rudolf **Werckmeister**, in Oranienburg, also in Berlin, 1802–09. Plesske 672.

Carl **Zulehner**, in Mainz, 1802–1827.

Friedrich **Hofmeister** (with one f), in Leipzig, founded 1807. Plesske 371–89. See Figure 153.

Adolf Martin **Schlesinger**, in Berlin, 1810–1864. Plesske 460–73. See Figures 164–5.

ANDRÉ EDITIONS. *Figure 144 (top):* c.1784. *Figure 145 (right):* c.1807. *Figure 146 (bottom):* 1820. The latter two are lithographed.

August Heinrich **Cranz**, in Hamburg, founded 1814. Plesske 294–5. See Figures 158–9.

Anton **Böhm** & Sohn, in Augsburg, founded 1815. Plesske 164–7.

A. **Benjamin**, in Altona, founded 1818. Plesske 154–9.

Adolf **Nagel**, in Hannover, founded 1819. Plesske 504–6.

Traugott **Trautwein**, in Berlin, 1820–1902. See Figure 161.

Heinrich Albert **Probst**, in Leipzig, 1823–1836; succeeded by F. Kistner, 1836–1846; **Kistner & Siegel**, since 1846. Plesske 428–40. See Figure 154.

J. **Aibl**, in Munich, 1825–1904. See Karl Ventzke, "Zur Frühgeschichte des Musikverlags Joseph Aibl in München," *Die Musikforschung*, 25 (1972), 316–7.

Julius **Schuberth**, in Hamburg, founded 1826, also later in Leipzig. Plesske 597. See Figure 162.

F. **Pustet**, in Regensburg, founded 1826. Plesske 537.

K.F. **Heckel** & successors, in Mannheim, founded 1826.

G.M. **Meyer**, in Braunschweig, 1826–1856. See Figure 163.

Henri **Litolff**, in Braunschweig, founded 1828. Plesske 474–80.

Bote & Bock, in Berlin, founded 1838. Plesske 181–204. See Figure 160.

D. PLATE NUMBERS: German publishers used plate numbers extensively. These are particularly useful in dating, since street addresses were generally omitted. Several German publishers assigned numbers to a text rather than an edition, however, so that the same number would appear on all editions of the same music. Others, such as Breitkopf & Härtel, maintained several plate number series at one time for engravings, type-set editions, and lithographs.

Special sources include the following:

Otto Erich Deutsch, *Musikverlagsnummern* (Berlin 1961).

Martin von Hase, "Musikverlagsnummern," *Der Musikhandel*, 13 (1962), 208–9.

SOUTH GERMAN EDITIONS AROUND 1850. *Figure 147 (top)*: Munich: Falter, c.1840. *Figure 148 (left)*: Mainz: Schott, 1843. *Figure 149 (bottom)*: Mainz: Schott, 1855.

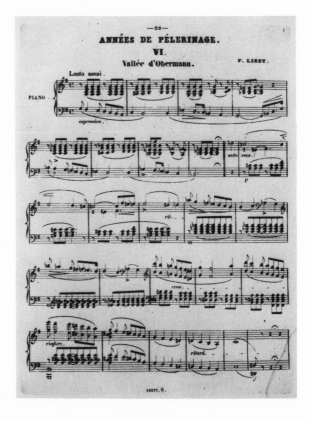

Cards for all RISM entries from West German libraries with German and foreign plate numbers up to c.1820 have been used to prepare a plate-number file which is maintained by the Deutsche Arbeitsgruppe of RISM, in the Bayerische Staatsbibliothek, Munich.

A file is also maintained by Dr. F.W. Riedel in Mainz (Musikwissenschaftliches Institut, Johannes Gutenberg-Universität, Saarstrasse 21, 6500 Mainz).

E. CATALOGUES: These will be covered in the forthcoming book by Liesbeth Weinhold & Alexander Weinmann, *Bibliographie der Verlags- und Sortimentskataloge im deutschsprachigen Raum bis zum 1850.*

F. COPYRIGHT: As early as 1829, a *Schutzverband gegen den Missbrauch des Nachdrucks von Musikalien* ("society for protection against the misuse of music reprinting") had been organized mainly through the efforts of Friedrich Hofmeister. This group, limited at first to Leipzig publishers, was expanded later to become the Verein der deutschen Musikalienhändler. Depository copies were stamped "Eingetragen in das Vereinsregister" (without a date, however), and sent to the Deutsche Bücherei in Leipzig. This arrangement served to reduce piracy but could not eliminate it. Not until 1901 was copyright law enacted in Germany. The published list of music deposited is the great Hofmeister series (see below), which continued up to 1903, when the Verband ceased to be concerned with copyright matters.

During the French occupation, 1795–1814, Simrock editions were sent to Paris, and have the marking "Enregistré à la Bibliothèque Nationale"; or, after 1804, "à la Bibliothèque Impériale"; or often simply the abbreviation, "P.D.L.E.E.A.L.B.I." ("Propriété de L'Éditeur, Enregistré à la Bibliothèque Impériale"). Depository copies are also extant in various German national libraries (i.e., **D:Bds, D:DS, D:F, D:Hs, D:HVl, D:KA, D:Kl, D:Mbs, D:MZu, D:S, D:WI**). Of these libraries, Stuttgart received copies from as early as 1817; most of the others, however, did not receive them until after 1900.

See Kurt Dorfmüller, "Die Bestellung von Musikalien im Leihverkehr," *Zeitschrift für Bibliothekswesen und Bibliographie*, Sonderheft 8 (1968), 62–5; the article "Pflichtablieferung" in Fritz Milkau & George Leyh, *Handbuch der Bibliothekswissenschaft*, 2. Auflage (Wiesbaden, 1952), v. 1, pp. 1000–5; also Karl-Heinz Köhler, "Die Musikabteilung," in *Die deutsche Staatsbibliothek* (Leipzig 1961), v. 1, pp. 241–74.

PETERS AND PRECURSORS. *Figure 150 (top)*: Keyboard music, 1801, issued by Kühnel jointly with Hoffmeister in Vienna. *Figure 151 (right)*: Kühnel song collection, c.1806. *Figure 152 (bottom)*: Peters song collection, c.1818.

G. ANNOUNCEMENTS: New music was announced in several early German periodicals and series, among them:

"Neuigkeiten" in Mizler's *Musicalischer Bibliothek* (1736).

"Nachrichten von Büchern [und Noten]" in Marpurg's *Historisch-kritischen Beiträgen* (1754–78).

"Briefe von alten und neuen Musikalien" in Marpurg's *Kritischen Briefen* (1759–1764).

"Ankündungen" in Eschstruth's *Musicalische Bibliothek* (1756).

"Anzeigen" in Hiller's *Wöchentliche Nachrichten* (1766–70).

"Anzeigen Neuerer Musikalien" in Koch's *Journal der Tonkunst* (1795).

Above all, Rochlitz's *Allgemeine musicalische Zeitung* (AMZ), from its beginnings in 1798, was supplemented by "Intelligenzblätter," given over to listings of new music from particular music publishers. In these irregular supplements, the titles were grouped, so that one batch of titles from a particular publisher might include new works as well as works which were first issued immediately after the last listing, often as much as several years previously. We suspect that the list might also include works which the publisher intended to issue but which had not yet appeared. Reviews of new music in the main body of the *AMZ*, on the other hand, offer a definite *terminus ante quem* for the publication.

Between 1775 and 1820, meanwhile, the Leipzig and Frankfurt fair catalogues included a special section on music. Twice a year (Ostermesse in the spring and Michaelismesse in the fall), new editions were exhibited at the fair and listed in the catalogues. These announcements, little known to scholars, are generally not so crucial in dating as *AMZ* notices. Furthermore, for purposes of assigning a particular year, the Ostermesse catalogues do no better than give an even-odds choice of two (that is, the item in question may have been published between October of the preceding year and Easter of the present year). On the other hand, a fair-catalogue entry is certain proof that a given work had actually been published, since the exhibition of copies at the fair is presumed. A transcript of the entries from these fair catalogues was planned around 1945 by a group of music librarians in Washington, D.C., under the leadership of Richard S. Hill. The typing of information onto cards was never completed, however.

186   In addition, various local newspapers listed new publications. Since the

LEIPZIG EDITIONS. *Figure 153 (upper left)*: Hofmeister, c.1815. *Figure 154 (upper right)*: Kistner, 1857. *Figure 155 (lower left)*: Peters, c.1842. *Figure 156 (lower right)*: Peters, 1857.

publisher was close by, these sources are generally considered to offer the most accurate information on precise publication dates of any of the sources of announcements.

H. DESIGN & PRINTING PRACTICE: In various ways, the decoration of title pages and the arrangement of the pages of text provide useful help in dating. Between 1770 and 1810, ornamental titles often mention the designer or engraver — sometimes even a date — usually in tiny and scarcely readable form, or buried in the ornamentation. After 1810, the ornamental title declined; cross-hatched outline letters, on clean and typographically conceived title pages, came to be replaced by excessively florid and even deformed ornamental letters, which by 1820 tried to achieve a three-dimensional effect. Horizontal lines came to be rounded between 1810 and 1820. Arabesques and flourishes filled more and more of the vacant space. The evaluation of such changes requires a penetrating study of the artistic conceptions of title pages, and this affords a comparison of their use. Decoration on dated first editions and issues offers a useful dating key in reference to later editions and issues.

In the musical notation itself, the form and style of signs, such as the keys and rests, are helpful in dating.

See Georg Kinsky, "Erstlingsdrucke der deutschen Tonmeister der Klassik und Romantik," *Philobiblon*, 7 (1934), 347—66; also Kathi Meyer-Baer, "Die Illustration in den Musikbüchern des 15.—17. Jahrhunderts," *Philobiblon*, 10 (1938), 205—12; also Jean Loubier, "Künstlerische Notentitel," *Kunst und Kunsthandwerk*, 9 (1906), 574—89; Wolfgang Matthäus, "Die Elemente des Titelblatts im 18. Jahrhundert," *Fontes artis musicae*, 12 (1965), 23—6; and Liesbeth Weinhold, "Musiktitel und Datierung," *Fontes artis musicae*, 13 (1966), 136—40.

J. PAPER: General studies are pursued by and coordinated through the Papierforschungsinstitut, located in the Gutenberg-Museum in Mainz, where a large watermark collection can be found. Another large collection has been established at the Hauptstaatsarchiv in Stuttgart by Gerhard Piccard: see his series below. Regional studies have been made of paper from Bavaria and Württemberg by Friedrich Hössle, and by others for Schaumburg, Thuringia, and the Palatinate. Research into German manuscript music paper is beginning to be published in such studies as Robert Münster & Robert Machold, *Thematischer Katalog der ehemaligen Klosterkirchen Weyarn, Tegernsee, und Benediktbeuern* (Munich 1970), pp.

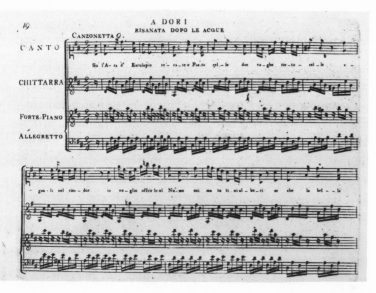

HAMBURG EDITIONS. *Figure 157 (top)*: Böhme, 1798. *Figure 158 (right)*: Cranz, c.1832. *Figure 159 (bottom)*: Cranz, c.1853.

164–76. Many watermarks have also been collected at the Bayerische Staatsbibliothek in Munich, in connection with the work on the RISM catalogues of music manuscripts and for the Deutsche Forschungsgemeinschaft. For further information, see Karl Theodor Weiss, *Handbuch der Wasserzeichenkunde* (Leipzig 1962); August Wilhelm Kazmeier, "Die regionale Entwicklung der Wasserzeichenforschung im Umriss dargestellt," *Gutenberg Jahrbuch*, 1950, pp. 25–30; Gerhard Piccard, *Die Wasserzeichenkartei Piccard im Hauptstaatsarchiv Stuttgart: Findbuch* (Stuttgart 1961–   ); and various other articles in the *Gutenberg Jahrbuch*.

K. CURRENCY & PRICING: Announcement of prices became common in music during the second half of the 18th century. After 1800, one sees the tendency to print only the name of the currency and to allow space for the exact amount to be either specially printed at the time of sale or entered in manuscript. Much of Germany consisted of small states and independent cities before 1871, but some of these had already by then renounced their own currency. As early as 1806 there was a trend to consolidation, which was furthered by political events in 1815, and again later by the conventions of Munich (1837) and Dresden (1839). The primary units were:

1. In Northern Germany, before 1837/1838:

> 2 Heller = 1 Pfennig
> 12 Pfennige = 1 (guter) Groschen
> 24 Groschen = 1 (Reichs) Thaler
> 2 Gulden = 1-1/3 Reichsthaler

2. In Northern Germany, particularly in Saxony and several other states, after 1837/1838:

> 12 Pfennige = 1 Groschen (Neugroschen)
> 30 Groschen = 1 Thaler

3. In Southern Germany before 1837/1838:

> 8 Heller = 4 Pfennige = 1 Kreutzer
> 24 Kreutzer Landmünze = 20 Kreutzer Conventionsmünze
> 120 Kreutzer Conventionsmünze = 2 Conv. Gulden = 1 Conv. Thaler

4. In Southern Germany after 1837/1838:

> 8 Heller = 4 Pfennige = 1 Kreutzer
> 60 Kreutzer = 1 Gulden
> 3-1/2 Gulden = 2 north German Thaler

NORTH GERMAN EDITIONS AROUND 1850. *Figure 160 (upper left)*: Berlin: Bote & Bock, c.1844.
Figure 161 (upper right): Berlin: Trautwein, c.1850. *Figure 162 (lower left)*: Hamburg, Schuberth, 1843.
An American copyright notice appears at the bottom of the page, above the plate number. *Figure 163
(lower right)*: Braunschweig: Meyer, c.1852.

SCHLESINGER EDITIONS FROM BERLIN. *Figure 164 (top):* c.1814. *Figure 165 (bottom):* 1830.

L. IMPORTANT COLLECTIONS: The major general collections are: (in B.R.D.) **D:B, D:Bhm, D:F, D:Hs, D:LÜh, D:Mbs, D:S1,** (In D.D.R.), **D:Bds, D:D1,** and **D:LEm.** Also very important, but particularly for holdings of music of the 16th and 17th centuries, are **D:As, D:Kl, D:MÜs, D:Rp,** and **D:W.** Important collections of the 18th-century nobility include **D:DO, D:HL, D:HR, D:LB, D:Rtt, D:WD,** and **D:BFb** and **D:RH** (the latter two now both in **D:MÜu**). Other major collections in the D.D.R. include **D:HAu, D:LEu, D:SWl,** and **D:Z.** The archives of publishers, such as André and Schott, are also important.

THE WHISTLING-HOFMEISTER CATALOGUES

NEIL RATLIFF

These bibliographies provide the most extensive listings of current published music ever compiled. Although in both the earliest years and in the late 1880's, international coverage was considerable, the Whistling-Hofmeister series include primarily music published in German-speaking countries. Among the major studies of the series are the following:

Rudolf Elvers & Cecil Hopkinson, "A Survey of the Music Catalogues of Whistling and Hofmeister," *Fontes artis musicae*, 19 (1972), 1—7.

Neil Ratliff, Introduction to the Whistling & Hofmeister, *Handbuch der musikalischen Litteratur: Reprint of the 1817 Edition and the Ten Nachträge (1818—27)* (New York, forthcoming).

Three series are involved: the *Handbuch der musikalischen Litteratur,* the *Musikalisch-Literarischer Monatsbericht* (now known as the *Deutsche Musikbibliographie*), and the *Jahresverzeichnis der deutschen Musikalien und Musikschriften.* Each one of these has had variant titles throughout its history: for details see the two previously cited writings.

Carl Friedrich Whistling initiated these lists when he issued his *Handbuch der musikalischen Litteratur* (1817) with the intention of presenting a list of music in print or generally in the stock of music dealers around 1816 (a controversial date). The coverage is fairly comprehensive retrospectively to about 1790; however, a few titles from as early as 1765 are cited. There were ten supplements to the original *Handbuch* between 1818 and 1827, the contents of which were cumulated into a "Zweite, ganz umgearbeitete, vermehrte und verbesserte Auflage" issued in 1828. This second edition also contains many, but not all, of the entries from the first edition. Some entries were revised because of changes in publisher (many Steiner titles in the 1817 edition, for instance, are assigned to Haslinger in the 1828), and some titles were omitted, since they were no longer available to the trade. The second *Handbuch*, like the first, covered only in-print or in-stock material. Three supplements to the second edition were published (1829, 1834, and 1839), and later cumulated into the so-called "Dritte Auflage" (1844—45). Again the same situation prevailed: All items from the second group of three supplements were included, but entries from the second edition which could no longer be obtained were deleted. A first supplement to the third edition appeared in 1852, and hereafter supplements continued to appear at five- to eight-year intervals until the demise of the *Handbuch* beginning in 1933.

The *Monatsbericht,* begun in 1829 and usually issued monthly, can be simply described as a list of new imprints, although its history is extremely complex. The *Handbuch*, which began with the 1829 supplement, is essentially a cumulation of the *Monatsbericht*. The *Monatsbericht* was cumulated into *Jahresverzeichnis* from the latter's inception to 1852, and all three continued to 1933. The *Jahresverzeichnis* and *Monatsbericht* still appear today, the latter as the *Deutsche Musikbibliographie*.

The Whistling-Hofmeister series is particularly important for verification of dates in conjunction with information derived from other known methods of dating. If it can be determined from other evidence that a piece of music was probably issued in the 1860's, one consults the *Handbuch* volume for 1860—67. If an entry is located there, one then searches through the yearly issues of the *Jahresverzeichnis*. When the entry is found in that source, generally the search is ended. Occasionally, however, it will be desirable to determine the exact month by referring to issues of the *Monatsbericht*. Unfortunately, the *Monatsbericht* often includes new issues of works published earlier; but even more deceptive are the occasional editions which were listed before publication.

Prior to 1852, one can find listings in Bartholf Senff's *Jahrbuch für Musik* (1842–1852), an annual bibliography unrelated to the Whistling-Hofmeister series but similar in format. For dates from 1829 through 1841, one must use the third edition of the *Handbuch* and the two previous supplements, and then search monthly lists just to determine the year of publication. After 1833, there are no cumulations of entries in the *Handbuch,* although one last, incomplete volume was published in 1843, covering "A" through "Linke."

Searches involving the early years are hampered by the classified arrangement of the entries, based on medium and form. Even though certain parts of the series use alphabetical composer entries, it was not until 1868 that this kind of access became a regular feature.

The complexities of the series are many, and a few additional matters must be mentioned. The original edition, prepared by Whistling, was reviewed in the *Allgemeine musikalische Zeitung* on June 25, 1817, in which the reviewer affirmed the importance of the list by way of pointing out many omissions. The fourth supplement (1821) is considerably larger than the previous ones because it contains many French publications which should have appeared in earlier supplements. With the founding of the Verein der deutschen Musikalienhändler in 1829, coverage was limited to editions issued by members of that organization. From 1840 through 1844 an unrelated monthly list called *Musikalischer Monatsanzeiger* was issued under the editorship of Fritz Whistling (Carl Friedrich's son). At this time the *Monatsbericht* was completely under the control of the Hofmeister Verlag. The systematic arrangements are different in these two series; a study carefully comparing them for accuracy and comprehensiveness remains to be done.

EARLY ARTARIA KEYBOARD
EDITIONS. *Figure 166 (top):*
c.1789. *Figure 167 (right):* c.1799.
Figure 168 (bottom): c.1814.

IX. *Austria*

A. SUMMARIES AND BIBLIOGRAPHIES: Among the foremost projects in any area of music bibliography are Alexander Weinmann's exhaustive and invaluable *Beiträge zur Geschichte des Alt-Wiener Musikverlages,* in two series: *Reihe 1* contains studies of particular composers; *Reihe 2* is devoted to particular publishers. The latter (cited in C. below) includes references to plate numbers, journal announcements, and other bibliographical information, but rarely provides any locations of extant copies or analysis of the copies, either bibliographical or textual. The plan of the series is discussed in Weinmann's "Zur Bibliographie des Alt-Wiener Musikverlages," *Festschrift Otto Erich Deutsch* (Kassel 1963), pp. 319–26.

Studies of German music publishing (cited in VIII. above) often include Austria as well. Especially important among the works cited there is Hans Martin Plesske, "Bibliographie des Schrifttums zur Geschichte deutscher und österreichischer Musikverlage," *Beiträge zur Geschichte des Buchwesens,* 3 (1968), 135–222.

For the early 18th century, see Hannelore Gericke, *Der Weiner Musikhandel von 1700 bis 1778* (Graz 1960).

B. DIRECTORIES: Alexander Weinmann, *Wiener Musikverleger und Musikalienhändler von Mozarts Zeit bis gegen 1860* (Vienna 1960; Weinmann *Beiträge* I, 5).

C. IMPORTANT NAMES (all in Vienna):

Anton **Huberty,** 1770–1778. Weinmann *Beiträge,* II, 7-A (1962).

Artaria & Cie., 1778–1858. Weinmann *Beiträge,* II, 2 (1952), revision in preparation. See also Plesske, items 130–4. See Figures 14–19, 166–8, 171, 178.

Christoph **Torricella,** 1781–1784(?). Weinmann *Beiträge,* II, 7-B (1962).

Franz Anton **Hoffmeister,** 1784–1806, after 1800 in partnership with Ambrosius **Kühnel** in Leipzig. Weinmann *Beiträge.* II, 8 (1964). See Figure 150.

Musikalisches Magazin, i.e., Leopold Koželuh, 1784–1802. Weinmann *Beiträge,* II, 1 (1950).

Josef **Eder,** 1787–1816, later in partnership with and succeeded by Jeremias **Bermann,** who was active to 1886. Weinmann *Beiträge,* II, 12 (1968).

Johann **Traeg,** 1794–1818. Weinmann *Beiträge,* II, 4 (1956).

K.K. Hoftheater Musikverlag, 1796–1822. Weinmann *Beiträge,* II, 6 (1961).

Tranquillo **Mollo,** 1798–1834. Weinmann *Beiträge,* II, 9 (1960). See Figures 169–70.

Ignaz **Sauer** ("Kunstverlag zu den sieben Schwestern"), 1798–1822; with Max Josef **Leidesdorf,** 1822–1827; Leidesdorf alone, 1827–1834/5. See Figure 172.

Carlo **Mechetti,** 1799–1810, succeeded by his nephew Pietro. Weinmann *Beiträge,* II, 10 (1966). See Figure 179.

Giovanni Cappi, 1801–1816, succeeded eventually by A.O. **Witzendorf,** 1842–1866. Weinmann *Beiträge,* II, 11 (1967). See Figures 174, 176.

Bureau des arts et d'industrie (Kunst- und Industrie-Comptoirs), 1801–1823. Weinmann *Beiträge,* II, 3 (1955). See Figure 175.

Chemische Druckerey of Alois Senefelder, later with S.A. **Steiner** & Rochus Kranitsky, 1803–1812; Steiner alone, 1812–1814, and with Tobias **Haslinger,** 1814–1826; Haslinger alone, after 1826. See Plesske, items 633–4. See Figure 180.

Ludwig **Maisch,** 1809–1816, and his successors, Daniel Sprenger, Mathias Artaria, &c. Weinmann *Beiträge,* II, 14 (1970).

Pietro Cappi, founded 1816, and Anton **Diabelli,** founded 1817, together 1818–1824; Diabelli with C.A. **Spina** thereafter; Spina alone after 1851 (but not using his name until 1857). See Figures 173, 177–8.

**MOLLO AND ARTARIA KEY-
BOARD EDITIONS.** *Figure 169
(top)*: Mollo, 1806. *Figure 170
(right)*: Mollo, 1801, possibly based
on Artaria plates (cf. Weinmann,
Artaria, p. 39; but note the plate
number 565 cited there. See also
Weinmann, *Mollo*, p. 18). *Figure
171 (bottom)*: Artaria, 1828.

Anton **Pennauer**, 1822–1835.

Minor publishers ("am Rande") are covered in Weinmann *Beiträge,* II, 13 (1970).

D. PLATE NUMBERS: Covered in the Weinmann *Beiträge.* For publishers not yet covered in this series, Deutsch *Musikverlagsnummern* is often helpful.

E. CATALOGUES: Covered in the Weinmann *Beiträge.*

G. ANNOUNCEMENTS: Covered in the Weinmann *Beiträge.* See also his "Die Wiener Zeitung als Quelle für die Musikbibliographie," *Anthony van Hoboken Festschrift* (Mainz 1962), pp. 153–60.

K. CURRENCY: Throughout the Austro-Hungarian Empire,

1 Kreutzer = 4 Pfennig = 8 Heller

During the period 1753–1857,

120 Convention Kreutzer = 144 Kreutzer Landmünz

= Convention Gulden = 1 Convention Thaler

1 Ducat = 2 Convention Thaler

In recent practice,

1 Schilling = 100 Groschen

See also Otto Erich Deutsch, "Austrian Currency Values and Their Purchasing Power, 1725–1934," *Music and Letters,* 15 (1934), 236–8.

L. IMPORTANT COLLECTIONS: A:Wn, A:Wgm, also the personal collections of Alexander Weinmann in Vienna, Anthony van Hoboken in Ascona, and Alan Tyson in London.

VIENNESE EDITIONS. *Figure 172
(top)*: Leidesdorf, 1827. *Figure 173
(center)*: Diabelli, 1829. *Figure 174
(bottom)*: Cappi & Czerny, c.1827.

VIENNESE EDITIONS. *Figure 175 (upper left):* Kunst- und Industrie Comptoir, 1802. *Figure 176 (upper right):* Witzendorf, 1853. *Figures 177 & 178 (bottom):* Diabelli, 1836 and 1850, the former showing serious cracks in the plates, the latter bearing a New York dealer's stamp of the late 1860s.

MECHETTI AND HASLINGER. *Figure 179 (upper left)*: Mechetti piano score, c.1839. *Figure 180 (upper right)*: Haslinger battle music, 1815. *Figures 181 and 182 (bottom)*: Haslinger editions, 1842 and 1859, with the distinctive use of parentheses for the plate number and an ownership statement below.

EDITIONS OF BERRA IN PRAGUE.
Figure 183 (top): Solo songs, 1815.
Figure 184 (left): Piano music, 1818. *Figure 185 (bottom):* Fugue collection, 1832.

X. *Czechoslovakia*

With Assistance of OLDŘICH PULKERT

C. IMPORTANT NAMES (all in Prague):

E. Schödl, fl.c.1810. See Figure 186.

Marco **Berra**, c.1815–c.1880? See Figures 183–5.

Johan **Hoffmann**, c.1835?–after 1860? See Figures 189–92.

K. CURRENCY: See Austria (IX. above).

M. OTHER EVIDENCE:

1. Several bibliographical studies are of special interest:

Vladimír Telec, *Staré tisky děl českých skladetelů* 18. století v Universitní knihovně v Brně (Prague 1969) covers music by Czech composers now in the University Library in Brno, some of it published in Czechoslovakia.

O.E. Deutsch, "Ein Prager Beethoven-Druck," *Der Auftakt,* 11 (1931), 45–8; cf. Kinsky & Halm, p. 526 (WoO 74).

2. Potentially valuable, but not yet extensively studied, are such documents as the inventories of collections, bequests, deliveries, and the like, preserved in the archives of various families, circles of the nobility, and musical organizations. Receipts from suppliers and correspondence with them are also important. Additional valuable information is to be extracted from the concert programs and other archival material of performing groups, notable among them being the early Carlsbad orchestra.

3. Censorship lists are also said to be particularly valuable in work with Czech music between 1800 and 1850. For a survey of this subject, see Julius Marz, *Die Österreichische Zensur in Vormärz* (Munich 1959), especially p. 64. Whenever a censor's office was located, records were kept. A project is now in progress, supervised through the archival offices in Prague, for transcribing these entries.

4. The massive Cumulative Music Catalogue, a union list for the whole country, will some day be extremely valuable. See the discussion by Dr. Pulkert in *Ročenka státní knihovny ČSR v Praze,* 1970, pp. 68–82.

MINOR PUBLISHERS FROM PRAGUE. *Figure 186 (top)*: Schödl piano music, 1810. *Figure 187 (right)*: Haas piano music. The punches used in these editions also may be seen in Berra editions: cf. Figures 183—4 above. *Figure 188 (bottom)*: Pluth solo songs, c.1820.

EDITIONS OF HOFFMANN IN PRAGUE. *Figure 189 (upper left)*: Song sheet, c.1842. *Figure 190 (upper right)*: Folksong collection, c.1845, with an unusually small page size and narrow border reminiscent of contemporary French editions (cf. Figure 114). *Figure 191 (lower left)*: Song sheet, c.1850. *Figure 192 (lower right)*: Religious music, c.1860.

HUNGARIAN EDITIONS. *Figure 193 (upper left)*: Táborsky & Parsch folk songs, shortly after 1860. *Figure 194 (upper right)*: Miller art song, c.1820. *Figures 195 and 196 (bottom)*: Rózsavölgyi piano music, the former c. 1850 (with Rózsavölgyi initials for the plate number), the latter 1863 (with Grinzweil initials).

XI. *Hungary*

ILONA MONA & ISTVAN KECSKEMÉTI

A. SUMMARIES: Ilona Mona, *Hungarian Music Publication, 1774– 1867: First Summary* (Budapest 1973), an invaluable work for the bibliographer which supersedes various articles by Kálmán Isoz.

C. IMPORTANT NAMES (all in Pest):

Weingand & Köpf, from Bavaria, published music between 1774 and 1785, emphasizing the music of local composers. Their successor, József **Eggenberger**, was active from 1802 until 1850; his son Ferdinánd continued to 1898.

János Sámuel **Liedemann** was active from 1786 until c.1818; his son Frigyes continued to 1822.

József **Leyrer**, was active after 1799, working closely with the Kunst und Industrie Comptoir in Vienna; but he went bankrupt in 1806 and gave up music selling. His successors were József **Schreyvogel** (1805– 1808), József **Riedl** (1808–1812, 1815–1822), Zsigmond **Rabus** (1812–1815), and Károly **Lichtl** (1822–1831), the latter important as a publisher in his own right.

Konrád Adolf **Hartleben**, was active from 1801 until he sold his shop to Lichtl in 1826; his pupil, Ferdinánd **Tomala**, was active from 1826 to 1842, and perhaps again much later.

Károly Tódor **Miller** (Müller), was active as a publisher between 1820 and the time of the flood in 1838. See Figure 194.

Vince **Grimm** was the partner of and successor to Lichtl, mainly an art dealer who operated the "Kunst und Industrie Comptoir" from 1831 to 1844.

József **Wagner**, a cellist born in 1791, was active as a publisher from 1839 to 1858, and specialized in current Hungarian music, including the first works of Erkel.

209

József **Treichlinger**, born in Vienna in 1807, entered partnership with Wagner in 1842. He sold his business in 1844 to Grimm, but resumed publishing and later became the main music publisher of his day, specializing in dance music but also issuing local serious works. A son, also named József, was active after 1854.

Rózsavölgyi és Társa, music publishers, dealers, and later concert managers, was founded in 1850 by Gyula Rózsavölgyi, son of the noted violinist and composer, Mark Rosenthaler, and by Norbert Grinzweil (Gisswein). In 1858 the firm succeeded Wagner. When Gyula Rózsavölgyi died in 1861, the firm was maintained by Grinzweil and became the leading Hungarian music publisher around 1900. The name is still in existence as a music retail store. See Figures 195–6.

For fuller information see Mona.

D. PLATE NUMBERS: Lichtl was the first to use numbers. His series was continued by Grimm, who added his initials to Lichtl numbers and extended the series for his own editions.

Treichlinger numbers are said to be consistent for purposes of dating:

1	106	before 1846	322	1855
	107	1846	352	1856
	132	1847	370	1857
154	175	1849	394	1858
	200	1851	409	1859
	266	1853	423	1860

Rószavölgyi numbers below 1691 are designated "R. & C.," and predate 1861. Later numbers are designated "N.G." or "G.N.," denoting the Grinzweil period, which began in 1861. Although the sequence has many exceptions and duplications, the following chronology can be proposed:

25	1851	203	1856
86	1852	232	1857
126	1853	249	1859
133	1854	628	1860

For fuller information see Mona. See also János Demény, "Székely Imre életműve a lemezszám-kutatás tükrében" ("The Life Work of Imre Székely as Reflected by Recent Results in Identifying Plate Numbers"), in *Magyar Zenetörténeti Tanulmányok: Szabolcsi Bence 70.Születésnapjára* (Budapest 1969), pp. 201–14, 408.

J. PAPER: See Dorrit Somfai-Révész, "Wasserzeichen-Liste der Papiere in unserem Quellenmaterial," in Dénes Bartha & László Somfai, *Haydn als Opernkapellmeister; Die Haydn-Dokumente der Esterházy-Opernsammlung* (Budapest 1960), pp. 435–51.

K. CURRENCY: See Austria (IX. above).

L. IMPORTANT HOLDINGS: H:Ba, H:Bb, H:Bl, H:Bn, H:BA, H:SFmS, H:SP

The relationship between Hungarian musicians and Viennese publishers is discussed in Alexander Weinmann, "Magyar muzsika a bécsi zeneműpiacon; Bibliográfiai kíesérlet," in *Magyar Zenetörténeti Tanulmányok: Szabolcsi Bence 70. Születésnapjára* (Budapest 1969), pp. 131–77.

EARLY POLISH KEYBOARD EDITIONS. *Figures 197 (top) and 198 (left)*: Polonaises written and published by Elsner, 1803, and by Cybulski, c.1806. *Figure 199 (bottom)*: Brzezina tutor, 1829.

XII. *Poland*

MARIA PROKOPOWICZ

A. SUMMARIES & BIBLIOGRAPHIES: Maria Przywecka-Samecka, *Drukarstwo muzyczne w Polsce do końca XVIII wieku* (Kraków 1969), covers mostly the period before engraving, but does extend to 1800.

Tadeusz Frączyk, "Litografie i księgarnie," in his *Warszawa młodości Chopina* (Kraków 1961), pp. 235—307.

Maria Prokopowicz, "Musique imprimée à Varsovie, 1800—1830," in *The Book of the First International Musicological Congress devoted to the Works of Chopin* (Warsaw 1963), pp. 593—7; also her "La Musique imprimée de 1800 à 1831 comme source de la culture musicale polonaise de l'époque," *Fontes artis musicae*, 14 (1967), 16—22; also her "Z działalności warszawskich księgarzy i wydawców muzycznych w latach 1800—1831," in *Szkice o kulturze muzycznej XIX w.* (Warsaw 1971), pp. 33—49; also her "Wydawnictwo muzyczne Klukowskich 1816—1858" in *Rocznik Warszawski* (Warsaw 1974).

Krzysztof Mazur, "Polskie edytorstwo muzyczne między powstaniem listopadowym a styczniowym," in *Szkice o kulturze muzycznej XIX w.* (Warsaw 1971), pp. 51—89, is concerned with the period 1831—1864.

Władysław Hordyński, *Katalog polskich druków muzycznych, 1800—1863,* is eventually to include all editions of Polish music which appeared between 1800 and 1863, arranged by libraries. Vol. 1 (Kraków 1968) is between 1800 and 1863, arranged by libraries. Vol. 1 (Kraków 1968) is devoted to the University Library in Poznań and the Library of the Polish Academy of Science at Kórnik.

C. IMPORTANT NAMES:

NOTE: Polish publishers, engravers, and lithographers need to be differentiated, since several are often named in the same edition.

Publishers in Warsaw:

Jan **Engel**, ul. Krzywe Koło 1771/72–1776, in 1776 ul. Kamienne Schodki.

Józef **Elsner**, 1803–1805. See Figure 197.

Izydor Józef **Cybulski**, Nowe Miasto No. 1883, 1805–c.1818. See Figure 198.

Franciszek **Klukowski**, ul. Miodowa 489, 1816–6 February 1830; his heir Ignacy Klukowski to 1858. See Figure 203.

Ludwik **Letronne**, ul. Podwale No. 497a, 1819–1821, ul. Miodowa No. 497, in 1821; Krakowskie Przedmieście No. 456 naprzeciw Uniwersytetu, in 1822; ul. Miodowa No. 495, in 1823. See Figure 200.

Antoni **Brzezina**, ul. Senatorska No. 467 from 5 August to 1 October 1822, ul. Miodowa No. 481, 1822–1831; his partner and successor, Gustaw **Sennewald**, 1832–September 1905. See Figures 199, 201–2.

Jan **Widrychiewicz**, ul. Miodowa No. 490, 29 November 1822–1824, Krakowskie Przedmieście No. 414, 1824–1825.

Karol Ludwik **Magnus**, ul. Miodowa No. 486-B, 1828–c.1835; widow Józefa Magnus, c.1835–1846. See Figure 204.

Franciszek **Spiess**, ul. Senatorska No. 467, c.1839–1848. See Figure 205.

Publishers in other cities:

Józef **Zawadzki**, in Wilno, 1805–1838; his heirs, 1838–1840.

Karol Antoni **Simon**, in Poznań, ul. Wodna No. 103, later at Stary Rynek No. 84, 1817–1841.

T.J. **Jenisz** (**Jaenisch**), in Kalisz, c.1830.

Engravers: (in Warsaw):

Antoni **Płachecki** (working in Warsaw with I.J. Cybulski, 1805–c.1818, with F. Klukowski, 1818–c.1825).

214   Jan **Fuss**, c.1820, in Warsaw and Wilno.

POLISH MUSIC LITHOGRAPHS. *Figure 200 (top)*: Letronne piano anthology, 1821. *Figures 201 (right) and 202 (bottom)*: Sennewald art songs and dance music, c.1845.

Lithographers, in Warsaw except as noted:

Daniel **Knusman**, fl. 1822.

Józef **Brunn**, 1826.

Aleksander **Braun**, fl. 1827–1829.

J. **Dąbrowski**, fl. 1828–1829.

Józef Leon **Wemmer**, 1829–1830.

Teodor **Vivier**, 1830–1831.

Franciszek **Piller**, in Lwów, c.1825–1833.

D. PLATE NUMBERS: A card file, particularly strong for the period c.1850–1900, is maintained in the music division of the Biblioteka Narodowa in Warsaw.

Józef Elsner numbers:

	10	: 1803
	20	: 1804
22	43	: 1805

Izydor Józef Cybulski numbers:

5	: 1805–6
46	: 1811
76	: 1812
114	: 1817

Franciszek Klukowski numbers:

44	78	: 1818
	128	: 1821
133	154	: 1822

E. CATALOGUES: Karol Antoni Simon, *Katalog muzykaliów własnego nakładu* (Poznań 1822).

Antoni Brzezina, "Nuty muzyczne," in *Katalog ksiag polskich znaydujących się w księgarni A. Brzeziny i Komp.* (Warszawa [1830]).

**POLISH TITLE-PAGE ILLUSTRA-
TION.** *Figure 203 (top):* Klukow-
ski, 1818. *Figure 204 (bottom):*
Magnus, c.1829. *Figure 205 (right):*
Spiess, c.1845.

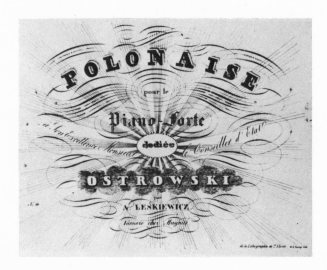

G. ANNOUNCEMENTS: New music was announced in several journals in Warsaw, Kraków, Lwów, Poznań and Wilno. Some of them are described in the series *Bibliografia muzyczna polskich czasopism niemuzycznych,* particularly in the first volume (Kraków 1962).

K. CURRENCY: Changes were frequent.

L. IMPORTANT COLLECTIONS: **PL**:Wn, **PL**:Wu, **PL**:Kj, **PL**:Pu, **PL**: KO, **PL**:Tu, also the Library of Warsaw Music Society.

XIII. *Denmark*

DAN FOG & NANNA SCHIØDT

A. SUMMARIES: General surveys include Erling Winkel, "Nodetryk: Danmark," in *Nordisk leksikon for bogväsen* (Copenhagen 1962), 2, 140–1; C. Nyrop, "Om nodetrykning i Danmark," *Skandinavisk Bog-trykker-Tidende,* 2 (1871), 140–2, 149–59; 3 (1872), 155–6; and V.C. Ravn, *Koncerter og musikalske selskaber i aeldre tid* (Copenhagen 1886; Festskrift i Anledning af Musikforeningens halvhundredeaarsdag, 1.). For earlier periods see E. Abrahamsen, *Liturgisk Musik i den danske Kirke efter Reformationen* (Copenhagen 1919); and Åke Davidsson, *Danskt Musiktryck intill 1700-talets mitt* (Uppsala 1962). Of particular importance are some of the antiquarian catalogues of Dan Fog, notably nos. 16 (*Bidrag til Dansk Musikhistorie,* 1954) and 244 (*Nordiske Komponister,* 1973).

B. DIRECTORIES: See Dan Fog, *Dänische Musikverlage und Noten-druckereien* (Copenhagen 1972).

C. IMPORTANT NAMES (all in Copenhagen):

Søren **Sønnichsen**, 1783–1826. See Figure 209.

C.C. **Lose**, 1802–1879, with various partners; successor to E.F.J. **Haly**, 1793–1802. See Figures 206–8.

Horneman, 1844–1879, at times with de Meza or Erslev.

E.O. **Friling**, 1799–1819, succeeded by C.D. Milde to 1861, others later.

Wilhelm **Hansen**, founded 1853.

Among minor publishers, Julius Cohen, C.G. Iversen were active after 1846, Th.C. Gandrup after 1849.

For further information see Fog, *Dänische Musikverlage.*

D. PLATE NUMBERS: In Det Kongelige Bibliotek, Copenhagen, a publishers' catalogue was established in the music department by the late Sven Lunn. It now covers all of the library's music except for some items either acquired since 1961 or not re-catalogued. See Fog, *Dänische Musikverlage* for an exhausting survey of the topic.

E. COPYRIGHT: No music copyright until 1912.

F. ANNOUNCEMENTS: A massive and invaluable index to Danish music publishing activity as recorded in journals and other sources was compiled by S.A.E. Hagen (1842–1927), the music publisher. This has been uncovered only recently in Det Kongelige Bibliotek (by the above respondents, as a result of the present project), and remains to be thoroughly explored.

In addition, the file of about 25,000 cards assembled by Sigurd Berg, and now in the Musikhistorisk Museum, Copenhagen, is very useful.

G. DESIGN & PRINTING PRACTICE: See Kay Schmidt-Phiseldeck, "Om nodetitler," *Bogvennen,* (1929), 177–218.

J. PAPER: Ove K. Nordstrand, *Danmarks aeldste papirmøller og deres vandmaerker* (Copenhagen 1961; *Det Forenede Papirfabrikker*).

K. CURRENCY: The system before 1875 was based on the following:

> 1 Mark = 16 Skilling
> 1 Rigsdaler = 6 Mark

Since 1875, the present system of Kroner and Ører has been in effect.

L. COLLECTIONS: D:Kk.

COPENHAGEN EDITIONS. *Figure 206 (top)*: Ballet score, c.1807. *Figures 207 (left) and 208 (bottom)*: Lose piano music, 1823 and 1831.

EARLY SCANDINAVIAN EDITIONS.
Figure 209 (top): Sønnichsen oratorio, 1789, set in type and based on Breitkopf models (cf. Figure 118). *Figure 210 (right)*: Swedish Haydn edition, 1791. *Figure 211 (bottom)*: Müller lithograph, Stockholm c.1825.

XIV. *Sweden*

AXEL HELMER & CARI JOHANSSON

A. SUMMARIES: Carl Björkbom, "Svenskt musiktryck: Några anteckningar om musiktrycket under äldre tidersärskilt i Sverige," *Nordisk boktryckarekonst,* 2 (1937), 53–63.

Axel Helmer, *Något om musikaliedatering* (Svenskt musikhistoriskt arkiv, Bulletin IV, 1969), is an invaluable reference work which contains a general introduction as well as other features, as noted below.

See also A. Wiberg, *Den svenska musikhandelns historia* (Stockholm 1955).

B. DIRECTORIES: Helmer, *Något om musikaliedatering,* contains a "Litet förläggarlexikon" ("Brief Directory of Publishers"), pp. 9–13. See also his report in *Fontes artis musicae,* 14 (1967), 31–3.

C. IMPORTANT NAMES (all in Stockholm):

E.W. **Björkman**, founded 1837/38.

J.L. **Ebeling**, 1822–1824 and 1827–1835 (his firm had been sold to and was owned by J.F. Walter, 1825–1827).

Fehr & Müller, 1818–9; C. Müller, 1819–1832. See Figure 211.

Kongl. Privilegierade Musikaliska tryckeriet, 1783–1835 (O. Åhlström).

J.C. **Hedbom** (later "& Cie."), 1827–1852.

W.F. **Holmgren**, 1823–1824.

Rylander & Comp., 1849–1855; Rylander & Svanberg, 1852–1855.

Abr. **Hirsch**, founded 1838, and working under the name of Östergren-Hirsch prior to 1842.

Abr. **Lundquist**, i.e., Caron & Lundquist, 1838–1844; Lundquist alone, 1844–1849; with Rylander, 1849–1856; Lundquist alone, after 1856.

D. PLATE NUMBERS: (Helmer, p. 21ff.)

Hirsch (Östergren) numbers:

1	254 :	before 1849	633	700 :	1855
255	379 :	1849	701	758 :	1856
392	450 :	1850	759	815 :	1857
451	483 :	1851	817	875 :	1858
484	517 :	1852	879	959 :	1859
518	571 :	1853	960	1012 :	1860
574	632 :	1854			

Lundquist numbers:

1	300 :	before 1856
301	676 :	1856–1862

Elkan & Schildknecht numbers (not necessarily chronological: see Helmer):

1	11 :	1859
12	46/53:	1860

E. CATALOGUES: Helmer, pp. 14–20, contains a chronologically arranged list of "Förlagskataloger 1794–ca.1900."

F. COPYRIGHT (i.e., Royal Privilege): Olof Åhlström's *privilegium exclusivum* was valid for the period 1788–1823, although certain limitations of the privilege had been introduced by 1818. See A. Wiberg, "Striden om Olof Åhlströms musiktryckeriprivilegium," *Svensk tidskrift för musikforskning*, 34 (1952), 84–110. The privilege was not cited on the music except through the imprint designation, "Kongl. privilegierade musikaliska tryckeriet."

G. ANNOUNCEMENTS: The following Stockholm journals contain announcements: *Post & Inrikes Tidningar*, 1722–1825; *Stockholms Posten*, 1778–1833; *Dagligt Allehanda*, 1767–1859; *Extra Posten*, 1792–1795; *Aftonbladet*, 1830– .

There is a large collection of excerpts, prepared by A. Wiberg, on deposit at the Svenskt Musikhistoriskt Arkiv (Swedish Archives of Music History) in Stockholm.

H. DESIGN & PRINTING PRACTICE: Extensive and very important studies of the music typography of earlier periods have been prepared by Åke Davidsson. See, for instance, his *Studier rörande svenskt musiktryck före år 1750* (Uppsala 1957; Studia musicologica upsaliensia, 5.), and "Das Typenmaterial des älteren nordischen Musikdrucks," *Annales Academiae Regiae Scientiarum Upsaliensis,* 6 (1962), 76–101.

J. PAPER: Significant work has been done with several major collections, mostly of manuscripts. See Ingmar Bengtsson & Ruben Danielson, *Handstilar och notpikturer i Kungl. Musikaliska akademiens Romansamling* (Uppsala 1955; Studia musicologica upsaliensia, 3.); also Bruno Grusnick, "Die Dübensammlung; Ein Versuch ihrer chronologischen Ordnung," *Svensk tidskrift för musikforskning,* 46 (1964), 27–82, 48 (1966), 63–186; and Jan Olof Rudén's useful dissertation, *Vattenmärken och musikforskning; Presentation och tillämpning av en dateringsmetod på musikalier i handskrift i Uppsala universitetsbiblioteks Dübensamling* (Uppsala 1968).

K. CURRENCY:

pre 1776 :	1 daler silvermynt (d. smt), or from 1604 riksdaler (rdr smt) = 4 mark = 32 öre. 1 öre = 24 penningar. The price is normally given in d. smt, öre, and penningar.
1624–1776 :	also 1 daler kopparmynt (d. kmt).
1776–1855 :	1 riksdaler (after 1830, rdr specie) = 48 skilling; 1 skilling = 12 runstycken.
1855–1873 :	1 riksdaler riksmynt (rdr rmt) = 100 öre.
1873ff. :	1 krona (kr.) = 100 öre.

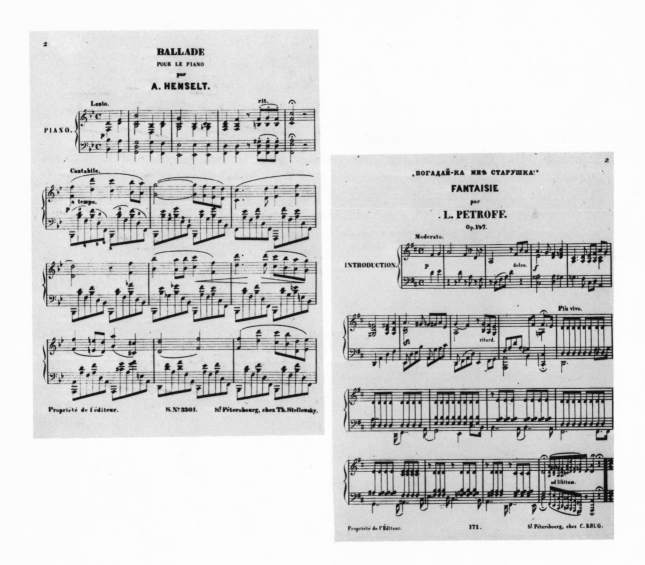

RUSSIAN PIANO EDITIONS. *Figure 212 (left):* Stellowsky, c.1850. *Figure 213 (right):* Krug, c.1860.

XV. *Russia*

A. SUMMARIES: Georgy Ivanov, *Notoiezdatelskoe delo v Rossii: Istoricheskaya spravka* (Moscow 1970), a general reference book with bibliographical citations.

Boris Volman, *Russkie pechatnye noty XVIII veka* (Leningrad 1957), also his *Russkie notnye izdaniya, XIX- nachala XX veka* (Leningrad 1970).

B.J. Yorgenson, *Ocherk istorii notopechataniya* (Moscow 1928) includes a general outline of the history of Russian music printing, pp. 33–41, 169ff.

Richard Schaal, "Zur Geschichte des russischen Musikschrifttums," *Das Antiquariat*, 9 (1953), 2–4.

B. DIRECTORIES: Cecil Hopkinson, *Notes on Russian Music Publishers* (London 1959). This author's John Field bibliography is also useful for information on Russian publishing.

C. IMPORTANT NAMES (all in St. Petersburg):

Johann Daniel **Gerstenberg**, 1793–1799. See Walter Gerstenberg, "Aus Petersburger Anfängen des Verlegers Johann Daniel Gerstenberg (1758–1841)," *Musik und Verlag* (Vötterle Festschrift; Kassel 1968), pp. 293–8.

Carl **Lissner**, 1795–1824.
Dalmas, 1800?–1829.
Ivan Karl **Paez** (Petz), 1810–1826.
Feodor **Stellovsky**, 1840–1876. See Figure 212.

The major firms of importance later all date from the end of the period of this study, i.e., Gutheil (Moscow, founded 1859), Jurgenson (Moscow & St. Petersburg, active after 1867), Bessel (St. Petersburg, founded 1869), and Belaieff (Leipzig, founded 1885).

D. PLATE NUMBERS: For Jurgenson plate numbers (after 1860), see Fuld, pp. 66–7.

PHILADELPHIA AND BOSTON EDITIONS BEFORE 1800. *Figures 214 and 215 (top):* Carr in Philadelphia. *Figure 216 (lower left):* Willig in Philadelphia. *Figure 217 (lower right):* Von Hagen in Boston.

XVI. *United States*

**D.W.K., ASSISTED BY DENA J. EPSTEIN,
RICHARD JACKSON, & WILLIAM LICHTENWANGER**

A. SUMMARIES AND BIBLIOGRAPHIES: William Arms Fisher, *150 Years of Music Publishing in the United States* (Boston 1933), pp. 23–62, is a brief historical survey, now out of date.

Ernst C. Krohn, *Music Publishing the Middle Western States Before the Civil War* (Detroit 1972; Detroit Studies in Music Bibliography, 23), covers seven cities.

G. Thomas Tanselle, *Guide to the Study of United States Imprints* (Cambridge 1971) includes numerous music publishers. See the discussion by D.W. Krummel in the *Yearbook for Inter-American Musical Research*, 8 (1972), 137–46.

Oscar Sonneck, *Bibliography of Early Secular American Music,* revised by William Treat Upton (Washington 1945; reprinted New York 1968) describes and locates about 1,500 18th-century editions.

Richard J. Wolfe, *Secular Music in America, 1801–1825* (New York 1964), covers about 10,000 editions and supersedes the lists for Boston by H. Earle Johnson (*Musical Interludes in Boston,* New York 1943) and for Philadelphia by D.W. Krummel, as well as includes new titles and corrections for Sonneck-Upton.

The Board of Music Trade, comprising at the time a membership of twenty of the country's largest music publishers, issued a *Complete Catalogue of Sheet Music and Musical Works* (1871). Its brief entries notwithstanding, this is a rather useful record of the music in print at that time, in all a total of at least 80,000 items. Dena J. Epstein has provided a valuable introduction to the facsimile reprint of this book (New York 1973) which describes music publishing circumstances of these years and those immediately following.

B. DIRECTORIES: Harry Dichter & Elliott Shapiro, *Early American Sheet Music, Its Lure and Lore* (New York 1941), includes a "Directory of Early American Music Publishers, 1768–1889," pp. 165–248. Although valuable for its day, it is now in need of updating. Modern directories of the early book trade in particular cities have also been prepared, a number of them issued by the New York Public Library.

C. IMPORTANT NAMES: Although music was issued in the American colonies throughout most of the 18th century, no great quantity was published until after 1786, and no music publishers were at all successful until 1793. Among the major publishers are the following:

James **Hewitt**, in Boston and New York, 1793–c.1825; his son James to c.1847. See Figures 219, 231.

Joseph **Carr**, in Baltimore, and his son Benjamin, mostly in Philadelphia, 1794–c.1820. See Virginia Larkin Redway, "The Carrs, American Music Publishers," *Musical Quarterly,* 18 (1932), 150–77. See Figures 213, 215.

George **Willig**, in Philadelphia, 1794–1856. See Figures 214, 236.

Gottlieb **Graupner**, in Boston, 1796–1835. See Figure 226.

George E. **Blake**, in Philadelphia, 1802–c.1850. See Figure 225.

Firth, Hall, & Pond, in various combinations, in New York, c.1827–c.1875. See Figure 237.

Oliver **Ditson**, in Boston, 1833–1937.

William C. **Peters** and other members of his family, in Louisville, Cincinnati, Baltimore, St. Louis, and New York, 1842?–1875. See Krohn, pp. 15–23.

Lee & Walker, in Philadelphia, 1845–1875.

Balmer & Weber, in St. Louis, c.1846–1907.

Root & Cady, in Chicago, 1858–1871. See Dena J. Epstein, *Music Publishing in Chicago Before 1871* (Detroit 1969; Detroit Studies in Music Bibliography, 14).

EARLY NEW YORK EDITIONS. *Figure 218 (upper left):* Peter Erben, c.1801. *Figure 219 (upper right):* Hewitt, 1799. *Figures 220 and 221 (bottom):* Paff, c.1801 and c.1807.

D. PLATE NUMBERS, by way of a revision of the report in *Fontes artis musicae,* 14 (1967), 33—7, based largely on a survey by Wilbur Jones of the copyright deposits in the Library of Congress (class M 1.A12; see F. below):

John Aitken, Philadelphia

1	311	:	1806—1811 (apparently not arranged chronologically)

Allyn Bacon (Bacon & Hart), Philadelphia

4	26	:	c.1816	131	170	:	c.1819
27	90	:	c.1817	171	200	:	c.1820
91	130	:	c.1818				

Balmer & Weber, St. Louis

1	31	:	1848 or earlier
	38	:	1849

Frederick Benteen, Baltimore

197	307	:	1843	1023	1151	:	1847
290	525	:	1844	1129	1438	:	1848
499	705	:	1845	1378	1631	:	1849
716	1019	:	1846	1632	1772	:	1850

See also Miller & Beacham

Silas Brainard, Cleveland

1788	:	1851
2214	:	1860

John Cole, Baltimore

A—Z		:	c.1822
2	104	:	c.1824
105	189	:	1825?

Oliver Ditson, Boston (see the Example in the Synopsis, II.A.1. above).

1011	1057	:	1845	1795	2188	:	1850
1086	1237	:	1846		2236	:	1851
1211	1449	:	1847		2693	:	1852
1439	1651	:	1848		14447	:	1857
1636	1830	:	1849		20268	:	1860

John Firth, New York; also Firth & Hall; also Firth, Hall, & Pond:

	206	:	1843
	2986	:	1844
3776	3858	:	1845
3887	4064	:	1846
4066	4227	:	1847

Firth & Pond, New York

3	270	:	1848	3283	3432	:	1855
193	675	:	1849		3714	:	1856
571	912	:	1850	4275	4321	:	1857
989	1020	:	1851	4395	4492	:	1858
	2589	:	1853	4552	4640	:	1859
2664	3059	:	1854	4677	5012	:	1860

J., A., & W. Geib, New York

No.2(4–6)–No.11(32–33): 1817?
| 83 | 84 | : | 1817? |

S.T. Gordon, New York

566	:	1851
1810	:	1856
4443	:	1858

Gottlieb Graupner, Boston

1	500	:	various dates
502	520	:	1814–1819

Wm. Hall & Son, New York

11	282	:	1848	997	1456	:	1851
307	550	:	1849	1620	1769	:	1852
564	951	:	1850	1892	2081	:	1853

Uri K. and Frederick Hill, New York (engravers)

| 4 | 45 | : | 1815–1816 |

Charles E. Horn, New York

143	209	:	1840
210	222	:	1841

233

Samuel C. Jollie, New York

10	:	1850

Charles H. Keith, Boston

122	200	:	1843
204	292	:	1844
	379	:	1845
453	456	:	1846
	480	:	1847

John G. Klemm (Klemm & Bro.), Philadelphia

1	200	:	1823 (Allyn	620	654	:	1844
			Bacon plates)	649	687	:	1845
201	260	:	c.1824	738	748	:	1846
	261	:	1826	760	785	:	1847
	548	:	c.1836	787	819	:	1848
	592	:	1839	823	830	:	1849

Lee & Walker, Philadelphia

	8	:	1844
10	45	:	1845
74	220	:	1846
219	379	:	1847
381	601	:	1848
604	822	:	1849
824	970	:	1850

Francesco Masi, Boston

13	46	:	c.1815

W.H. Oakes, Boston

42	62	:	1841
202	251	:	1847
274	332	:	1848
374	396	:	1849

Miller & Beacham, Baltimore (successors to Benteen)

1754	1903	:	1850
2017	2150	:	1851
2264	2371	:	1852

A & J. P. Ordway, Boston

2	50	:	1848
1059	1580	:	1850

James G. Osbourn, Philadelphia

	20	:	1831		395	:	1844
	25	:	1837	420	547	:	1845
167	197	:	1839	405(?)	545	:	1846 (?)
	200	:	1840		567	:	1848
	342	:	1843				

W.C. Peters, Cincinnati, &c.

	365	:	1846
1119	1120	:	1847
1137	1226	:	1848
1405	1489	:	1850
	1833	:	1853

Henry Prentiss, Boston

	28	:	1841
	315	:	1843
391	464	:	1844
	706	:	1850

George P. Reed, Boston

	4	:	184–?
	44	:	1841
1005	1014	:	1847
1015	1110	:	1848
1186	1524	:	1849
	2290	:	1856

John Siegling, Charleston

1	185	:	assigned after 1828 and probably not chronological

J.C. Smith, Philadelphia

	69	:	1829
	843	:	1841

George Willig, Jr., Baltimore

1437	1444	:	1843		2026	2075	:	1847
1850	1906	:	1844		2112	2159	:	1848
1921	1960	:	1845		2155	2258	:	1849
2012	2021	:	1846		2259	2359	:	1850

N.B.: Willig often assigned the same number to more than one edition.

Krohn, pp. 32–4, discusses the practice of "hyphenated numbering," i.e., following the plate number with a second number to indicate how many plates comprise the set (e.g., 294–6 tells us that there were six plates in the edition which bears plate number 294). See the Synopsis, II.B.3. above.

E. CATALOGUES: These were seldom issued, and the few extant copies have not been studied. See, however, the 1871 Board of Music Trade catalogue cited in A. above.

F. COPYRIGHT: Copyright was first enacted in 1783. Music was not recognized as a category until 1831, although musical editions before this date had occasionally been registered as books or as engravings. There is a significant increase in the amount of music copyrighted beginning in the years just before 1850. For a survey of the practices, see G. Thomas Tanselle, "Copyright Records and the Bibliographer," *Studies in Bibliography,* 22 (1969), 77–124.

Statements of copyright generally consist of the word "Copyright" followed by the date and the name of the claimant (e.g., "Copyright 1849 by Firth & Pond"). Occasionally in the years before 1830, the entire legal notice, beginning with the words, "Be it remembered," was copied. The copyright date is generally an accurate reflection of the publication date. Sometimes, however, publication was delayed: the copyright date may be as much as several years too early. Quite often new editions were prepared (i.e., new plates were made), on which the original copyright date was retained.

Music was copyrighted in the various U.S. District Courts before 1870. The record books of many of these courts are now preserved in the Rare Book Room of the Library of Congress. See Martin Roberts, *Records in*

AMERICAN SONG SHEETS: THE AGE OF FLORID CALLIGRAPHY. *Figure 222 (upper left):* c.1816. *Figure 223 (upper right):* 1824, with a copyright notice. *Figure 224 (lower left):* c.1830. *Figure 225 (lower right):* c.1830.

the Copyright Office Deposited by the United States District Courts Covering the Period 1790–1870 (Washington 1939). While there have been many scholars who have used these records, there is no transcript or index, either of the whole set or of the music, which comprises a remarkably large proportion of the total.

Extant depository copies are preserved in the Library of Congress, mostly in the bound volumes which make up class M 1.A12 in the Music Division. Also in the Library is a collection of title pages which were required by law to be deposited before publication, as soon as formal publication was planned. On each depository copy and on each title page appears, in manuscript, the actual date of receipt, which of course may not be the date of publication. Some of the depository title pages belong to editions which are not otherwise known to be extant and may in fact never have been published.

G. ANNOUNCEMENTS: A number of journals and newspapers carry notices of music "to be issued" or "newly issued." The notices from before c.1830 have often been extracted and indexed on cards, now preserved in the Americana Collection of the Music Division of the New York Public Library. See Wolfe, p. xxii, as well as the information sheet on the "Americana Files" for the Library.

H. DESIGN & PRINTING PRACTICE: See D.W. Krummel, "Graphic Analysis," M.L.A. *Notes,* II, 16 (1959), 213–33.

Introduction of various printing methods, particularly for purposes of illustrating the covers of sheet music, offers a *terminus post quem.* Although lithography, for instance, was introduced in the United States around 1818, there are very few lithographed illustrations on music before 1827. Chromo-lithography is said to have been introduced in America in 1851 by the four Rosenthal brothers in Philadelphia (Harry Peters, *America on Stone,* p. 343). There are, however, a number of sheet music editions with chromo-lithograph covers which bear much earlier copyright dates. (It is possible, however, that the chromo-lithographs were added to late impressions and new issues.) The illustration of early sheet music, in Boston particularly, is discussed in David Tatham, *The Lure of the Striped Pig* (Barre, Massachusetts 1973). See also Dichter & Shapiro, and the several entertainly informative books by Lester S. Levy.

PATTERNS OF IMITATION IN AMERICAN SONG SHEETS, c.1825. *Figures 226–9.* The exact dates have not been determined, and hence the sequence can not be established.

L. IMPORTANT COLLECTIONS: US:Wc is preeminent. Material may also be found in other collections with special American sheet music files, such as the following: **US:N** (Shapiro), **US:Cn** (Driscoll), **US:WOa, US:AAc, US:PHf, US:BLl** (Starr), **US:BU** (Grosvenor Library), **US:NYcu** (Hunt), and the private collections of Lester S. Levy (Baltimore), Walter N.H. Harding (late of Chicago), and Harry Dichter (Atlantic City). The work of the National Sheet Music Association should also be cited.

Richard J. Wolfe's forthcoming study of early American music printers promises to be a major contribution to the literature of this subject.

AMERICAN VOCAL MUSIC OF THE 1830s. *Figure 230 (upper left)*: Bourne song sheet, New York c.1830. *Figure 231 (upper right)*: Hewitt glee collection, New York c.1834. *Figure 232 (lower left)*: Fiot song sheet, Philadelphia 1839. *Figure 233 (lower right)*: Meignen song sheet, Philadelphia 1836. The latter two bear dated copyright statements.

AMERICAN SONG SHEETS OF THE 1840s. *Figure 234 (upper left):* Boston 1842. *Figure 235 (upper right):* Boston c.1840. *Figure 236 (lower left):* Philadelphia c.1845. *Figure 237 (lower right):* New York c.1843.

XVII. *Canada*

HELMUT KALLMANN

A. SUMMARIES: Helmut Kallmann, "The Publication of Music," 1960, an article prepared for a symposium, unpublished.

B. DIRECTORIES: Mr. Kallmann has extensive personal research files. In addition, old city and trade directories are useful, although there is no bibliography listing or locating them. (The Canadian Music Publishers Association's *Directory* lists currently active firms only.)

C. IMPORTANT NAMES: Beginning after c.1845, the following men and firms, most of them primarily importers of instruments and sheet music, also appear occasionally as publishers: A. & S. Nordheimer, in Toronto; Robert **Morgan**, in Quebec; Henry **Prince**, A.J. **Boucher**, both in Montreal; J.L. **Orme** & Son, in Ottawa; and Peter **Grossman**, in Hamilton. Music was also issued occasionally by the Montreal book publishers John Lovell and Eusèbe Senécal, as well as by the Toronto branch, formerly named Lovell & Gibson.

D. PLATE NUMBERS: The Canadian Music Library Association has prepared a data sheet project listing publications issued prior to 1921. Of some six thousand items catalogued so far, perhaps two hundred have plate numbers, which are indicated but not organized apart from the main composer-alphabet sequence. The project is described in *The Canadian Composer,* 11 (October 1966).

E. CATALOGUES: Music publishing was at first largely an adjunct to music and instrument selling, and dealers would include other (non-Canadian) publishers' music along with their own. Many pieces of sheet music have thematic incipits of other publications or lists, usually numbered, of titles in series.

F. COPYRIGHT: Although copyright was not authorized in Canada until 1867, some earlier Canadian publications were entered in the United States, principally in New York. At least one copyright is known to have been entered before 1867 in the Provincial Legislature of Quebec; but if there are other instances, they are probably very few.

L. IMPORTANT COLLECTIONS: The largest public collections of Canadian printed music belong to C:On, comprising mostly copyright deposits, and C:Tp, including several hundred items. The private collection of Helmut Kallmann, now being integrated into the holdings of C:On, includes about eight hundred items. Smaller but also choice collections are owned by Alan Suddon in Toronto and Lawrence Lande in Montreal. The latter, described in a catalogue of the collection, has been presented in part to C:Mm.

XVIII. *Brazil*

A. SUMMARIES: Mercedes Reis Pequeno, "Imprensa musical," in *Musica no Rio de Janeiro Imperial* (catalogue of an exhibition at the National Library; Rio de Janeiro 1962), pp. 66–81. Early music journals are discussed in Luis Heitor Corrêa de Azevedo, "Periódicos musicais no Brasil," in *Resenha musical* (a journal published in Araraquara, São Paulo, July–September 1939), pp. 3–5; also in Barão do Ramiz Galvão, *Catálogo da Exposição de História do Brasil* (Rio de Janeiro 1881–3), a general catalogue in which music journals are cited in the section on "Periódicos." (A large part of the music published in early Brazil, it will be seen, was issued in periodical series.)

C. IMPORTANT NAMES (all in Rio de Janeiro):

Charles H. **Furcy**, Pedro **Plancher**, and F.A. **Chénet** were active around 1820, but their work does not survive. The earliest extant music printed in Brazil dates from c. 1833.

Pedro **Laforge**, 1834–1869, managed an "estamparia de música" at rua do Ouvidor 149, and printed several hundred editions, including popular songs ("modinhas") as well as such series as the *Delicias da jovem pianista* (1840), *Recreação da jovem fluminense* (1840), *Progresso da jovem pianista* (1842), *Prazeres do baile* (1843), *Grinalda da jovem pianista* (1845), and *Ramalhete dos principiantes* (1848). See Figure 240.

João Bartolomeu **Klier**, 1836–1855, publisher of the dance music collection, *Terpsichore Brazileira,* and an important music dealer.

Victor **Larée** and Eduardo **Laemmert**, lithographers after c.1834.

Frederico **Briggs**, active 1840–1843 as a lithographer.

Jorge Matias **Heaton** & Eduardo **Rensburg,** lithographers, 1840–1853, active at first at rua do Hospício 103, later at Rua do Ouvidor 35, still later at Misericordia 110, and eventually at rua da Ajuda 68, where they issued the popular periodical, *Ramalhete das damas.* The series, which included mostly operatic rather than native Brazilian music, lasted until 1850 and included around 130 pieces. See Figure 239.

J.J. **Rego,** a lithographer, who in 1842 issued four numbers of the series, *Philo-Harmonico,* and promoted the music of native Brazilian composers. See Figure 238.

Falleti & Cia., active beginning in 1846 at rua do Ouvidor 145, as publishers of the series for piano, *Flores melodiosas,* and for flute, *Orpheo Brazileiro.*

Isidoro **Bevilacqua,** 1846–1940, originally a music teacher and later a dealer, and at the end of the century one of the most important music publishers in Brazil.

Filippone & Cia., 1847–c.1884, at rua dos Latoeiros 59, publishers of *O Brazil Musical,* the most important of all the periodicals, as well as a number of other series. See Figure 241.

D. PLATE NUMBERS: For Filippone, the following assignments, taken mostly from *O Brazil Musical,* can be made:

1	15	:	1847
16	60	:	1848
61	118	:	1849
119	210	:	1850

E. CATALOGUES: Filippone & Cia. did use plate catalogues, but not until 1850. There is an 1837 catalogue issued by Müller & Heinen, who were music dealers and managers of a music lending library.

F. COPYRIGHT: Not in effect until 1898.

K. CURRENCY: Beginning in 1833, 1 milreis = 1000 reis

L. IMPORTANT COLLECTIONS: **BR:**Rn has, in the Music Section, a card catalogue listing the library's holdings of music printed in Brazil during the imperial period (1822–1889).

Beijo a maõ que me condena

MODINHA

Composta por o R.S.P.M.

JOSE MAURICIO NUNES GARCIA.

EARLY BRAZILIAN MUSIC PERIODICALS. *Figure 238 (upper left):* J.J. Rego lithograph, 1842. *Figure 239 (upper right):* Title page of the 1840s. *Figure 240 (lower left):* Laforge music from 1837. *Figure 241 (lower right):* Filippone title page used after 1848.

Post Script

INTERNATIONAL COMMERCE IN MUSICAL EDITIONS

Published music is generally intended for wide international circulation, more so probably than is true of most published books. Depending on the country involved and the extent of its music publishing industry, as well as the tastes of her musicians, as much as 90 per cent. and probably seldom less than 30 per cent. of the music sold within its boundaries comes from foreign publishers. There are several reasons for this. Musical notation is the same in all countries, while the standardized terminology is almost universally Italian. Musicians, however, have typically been able to use several languages. Many of them have studied abroad and travelled widely. Their reputations were established in various "capitols" of the "music world," reinforced in others of these same cities, and then promoted in the "provinces." Finally, music copyright was slow to be established, so that publishers found it advantageous to promote their editions abroad. As a result, published music has tended to be circulated widely, in particular from Leipzig but also from Berlin, Vienna, London, Paris, and Milan. The use in the present book of "National Reports" will thus slight the various kinds of international commerce, of which the following can be distinguished:

A. International Copyright Protection. See the Synopsis, IV.A., also the Example for IV.D.1.

NOTE: The best known major composers whose works were subject to simultaneous publication are probably Mendelssohn and Chopin. Surveying Maurice J.E. Brown, *Chopin: An Index of His Works* (2nd ed., New York 1972), for instance, we can observe that many works were issued in Leipzig by Breitkopf & Härtel, in Paris by Schlesinger, and also in London by Wessel. Sometimes the three editions appeared about the same time (as with nos. 64 or 118), sometimes nearly so (as with nos. 102 or 105, a month apart), but sometimes as much as five months apart (as with no. 41). Furthermore, the priority among the publishers will vary from work to work. See also Alan Tyson, *The Authentic English Editions of Beethoven* (London 1963), *passim.*, espeically Appendix II.

B. Foreign Branches of a Firm. Although most such branches date from around or after 1860 (such as Schott in Antwerp), a few important ones are of our period, mostly because of the emigrations of younger sons. Hummel in Berlin, Artaria in Milan, and Schlesinger in Paris are among the best examples of this. The international network planned by André just after 1800 is one of several such schemes devised by early promoters of lithography.

C. Migration of Music Engravers and Publishers. Among literally dozens of examples are the instances of Huberty moving from Paris to Vienna, Hoffmeister from Vienna to Leipzig, Riley and Stodart from London to New York, or Rieter-Biedermann from Winterthur to Leipzig.

D. Agents in Another Country. See the Synopsis, III.D.

E. Foreign Production. There are several kinds of relationships.

1. *Commerce in Engraving Work.* For instance, the first music published by Sønnichsen in Copenhagen, a work by Claus Schall around 1784, was issued from plates which were engraved in London, according to C. Thrane, *Fra Hofviolonernes Tid* (on the authority of Dan Fog).

2. *Commerce in Plates (Re-issue).* Hoboken has reported four instances involving music of Haydn. Artaria plates for the "Russian" quartets were sold to Napier in London, while those for the op.31 divertimento were sold by Artaria to Longman and Broderip. The Hummel plates for several keyboard sonatas were sold also to Longman. Hummel, in turn, used Pleyel plates (with Pleyel's plate number 305) for the op.46 quartets. See Anthony von Hoboken, "Probleme der musikbibliographischen Terminologie," *Fontes artis musicae,* 5 (1958), 12.

3. *Commerce in Sheets.* Three Haydn symphonies, nos. 79–81, were issued by Artaria with opus nos. 38–40. Sheets from these plates were sent to Leduc in Paris, who added his own title page but retained the numbers 38–40. We can be reasonably sure that the plates stayed in Vienna, since Artaria later issued the music with the opus number now changed to 40, nos. 1–3. The music was also re-issued later by Cappi and Mollo, using the op.40 designation. See H.C. Robbins Landon, *The Symphonies of Joseph Haydn* (London 1955), p. 729.

F. Piracy. Very little is known about this evasive matter: see the Synopsis, IV.D.3.c.

Illustrations

In the course of handling hundreds of different copies, bibliographers come to develop what they usually regard as a "sixth sense" about dates and other imprint information. They associate certain general appearances with periods and publishers; and they learn when to become suspicious on no firmer grounds than that a particular copy "looks" unusual. The study of bibliographical evidence (Synopsis, VI., especially VI.E.) may be viewed as largely an attempt to describe and to codify such matters, since the critical factors involved almost always turn out to be quite specific.

Most of the illustrations in this book were selected with the use of the Compiler's "bibliographical index" to the music collections in the Newberry Library. It would be important if one could claim that each of them was typical of its country, engraver, and date, for various specified reasons. Unfortunately, one can seldom do this. The output of most firms has never been arranged and examined as a whole, and thus those critical details have rarely been identified. The examples in this book represent, for now, the Compiler's "best guesses." One hopes they will serve to encourage further study.

Furthermore, it should be remembered that much detail is inevitably lost in reproduction. The texture of early paper, the visual characteristics of early inks, and the subtle effects which result when the two of them meet in the press, can never be re-created in photographs. In addition, most of the illustrations in this book are greatly reduced in size, as indicated in the list which follows (0.33 designating a copy here which is one third the size of the original). Full-size reproductions would naturally have been very desirable, but since most of the pages shown here run to 300 X 250 cm. and larger, reductions seemed necessary.

The copies are identified, located, and reduced as follows:

Pages	*Figures*

28 4. Giacomo Meyerbeer, *Le Prophète,* piano-vocal score (Paris: Brandus & Cie., [1848]), proof sheets with the composer's holograph corrections, page 15. Berkeley, University of California Music Library, M 1503 M35 P7 1848 Case X. Reduction 0.64.

29 5. Letter from Ludwig van Beethoven to his publisher, 6 May 1811. Bonn, Beethovenhaus, Sammlung H.C. Bodmer. Reduction 0.83.

33 6. Johann Baptist Cramer, *Saxon Air with Variations,* title page of the original edition (London: Chappell [1811]). British Museum, h.364.(33.). Reduction 0.39.

7. The same, later issue (London: Chappell [181–?]), title-page detail. British Museum, H. 3691.v.(2.). Reduction 0.65.

8. The same, with paste-over Mitchell imprint, title-page detail. British Museum, g.451.(3.). Reduction 0.65.

9. The same, later issue (London: Latour, [c.1827]), title-page detail. British Museum, g.443.u.(13.). Reduction 0.65.

10. Same as Figure 5 above, detail of the first page of music. Reduction 0.38.

11. Same as Figure 8 above, detail of the first page of music. Reduction 0.38.

37 12. Ludwig van Beethoven, *Christus am Oelberge,* the original vocal score (Leipzig: Breitkopf & Härtel [1811]), title page. Munich, Bayerische Staatsbibliothek, Musiksammlung, 2° 380.

13. The same, later vocal score (Leipzig: Breitkopf & Härtel [1821]), title page. Lübeck, Bibliothek der Hansastadt Lübeck, Mus A 121 d.

40 14. Wolfgang Amadeus Mozart, *Die Zauberflöte,* original piano score of the overture (Vienna: Artaria [1791]), p. 4. Bloomington, Indiana, Lilly Library, uncatalogued copy 1. Reduction 0.33.

15. The same, later state. Bloomington, Indiana, Lilly Library, uncatalogued copy 2. Reduction 0.33.

16. The same, later state. Bloomington, Indiana, Lilly Library, M 3.3 .M93 Z3. Reduction 0.33.

41 17. The same as Figure 14 above, p. 7.

18. The same as Figure 15 above, p. 7.

19. The same as Figure 16 above, p. 7.

77 20. *Encyclopèdie, ou Dictionnaire raisonné des sciences, des arts, et des métiers* (Paris 1751ff.), the supplementary volumes of *Planches,* Tome 7 (1767), in the section on "Imprimerie en taille douce." Urbana, University of Illinois Library, xq034 En1 1751.

80 21. Watermark copied by Jan LaRue from the copy of *Six simphonies . . . de différents auteurs* in Brussels, Conservatoire Royale de Musique. (RISM, B II, p. 383, there dated [1759]). Original size.

22. Watermark found in Croydon Parish Records, and supplied to Jan LaRue. Original size.

23. Watermark copied by Jan LaRue from the copy of Franz Beck symphonies in the Öffentliche Bibliothek der Universität Basel, Kr.IV.26. Original size.

81 24. Watermark copied by Jan LaRue from the manuscript of Joseph Weigl, *Il amor molinaro,* in Vienna, Österreichische Nationalbibliothek (Cod. 19355). Original size.

Pages   Figures

25. Watermark copied by Jan LaRue from the *Lliso de musica* (1778) in Barcelona, Biblioteca Orfeó Catalá. Original size.

26. Watermark copied by Jan LaRue from the manuscript (Cod. 17907) of music by Reinhard Keiser in Vienna, Österreichische Nationalbibliothek. Original size.

85   27. Broadside from Cambridge, Magdalene College, Pepysian Library.

87   28. Thomas Rowlandson, "Copper-Plate Printers at Work" (1785). Cf. Joseph Grego, *Rowlandson the Caricaturist* (New York 1880), v.1, p. 167.

89   29. "The Printer," in Edward Hazen, *Panorama of the Professions* (Philadelphia 1854), p. 180. Urbana, University of Illinois Library, 603 H338p.

30. "The Copperplate Printer," *ibid.*, p. 173.

31. "The Lithographer," *ibid.*, p. 175.

91   32. [Alessandro Scarlatti, &c.], *Songs in the Opera call'd Pyrrhus and Demetrius* (London: Walsh [1709?]). Newberry Library, Case VM 1505 S28p.

33. [Francesco Conti, &c.], *Songs in the Opera call'd Clotilda* (London: Walsh [1709]). Newberry Library, Case VM 1505 S28p.

34. *Songs in the Opera call'd Almahide* (London: Walsh [1710]). Newberry Library, Case VM 1505 S28p.

35. [Francesco Mancini], *Songs in the Opera call'd Hydaspes* (London: Walsh [1710]). Newberry Library, Case VM 1505 S28p.

36. [Carlo Francesco Cesarini, &c.], *Songs in the Opera call'd Love's Triumph* (London: Walsh [1708]). Newberry Library, Case VM 1505 S28p.

95   37. *Encyclopèdie, ou Dictionnaire raisonné des sciences, des arts, et des métiers* (Paris 1751ff.), the supplementary volumes of *Planches*, Tome 5 (1767), in the section on "Gravures en lettres, en géographie, et en musique." Urbana, University of Illinois Library, xq034 En1 1751.

97   38. Details from Felice Giardini, *VI soli a violino e basso, op.7* (London [1759]). Library of Congress. Original size.

39. Details from John Camidge, *Six Easy Lessons* (York: Thomas Harby [1764]). Library of Congress. Original size.

40. Details from Giuseppe Catanei, *VI sonate a violino e basso . . . , op.1* (London [1765]). Library of Congress. Original size.

41. Details from Samuel Babb, *Six Sonatas, op.1* (London: The Author [c.1770]). Library of Congress. Original size.

42. Details from Giovanni Mane Giornovichi, *A Favorite Sonata* (London: Longman & Broderip [1792]). Library of Congress. Original size.

43. Details from Ogilvy, *The Battle of Waterloo* (Edinburgh: Muir & Wood [1815?]). Library of Congress. Original size.

124   44. Alexander Lee, *The Bavarian Girl's Song, "Buy a Broom!"* (London: Mayhew [c.1825]). Newberry Library, Driscoll Collection.

128   45. Henry Purcell, *A Choice Collection of Lessons for the Harpsichord or Spinnet.* "Third Edition." (London 1705). Newberry Library, Case -VMT 252 P 98c. Reduction 0.54.

253

255

Pages   *Figures*

88. P.A. Corri [i.e., Arthur Clifton], *Divertimento alla Montanara* (La Haye: Weygand [18——]). Newberry Library, 8A 724. Reduction 0.38.

89. Johann Baptist Cramer, *Les menus plaisirs* (Brussels: Messemaeckers [18——]). Newberry Library, 8A 653. Reduction 0.38.

152   90. Esprit Philippe Chédeville, *IIe recüeil de contredances* (Paris: Chedéville [173–?]). Newberry Library, -VM 145 C 51c2. Reduction 0.41.

91. Jean Philippe Rameau, *Dardanus* (Paris: L'auteur [1739]). Newberry Library, VM 1500 R 17d. Reduction 0.43.

92. François André Danican Philidor, *Blaise le savetier* (Paris: la Chévardiere [1759]). Newberry Library, VM 1500 P 54b. Reduction 0.42.

155   93. Esprit Philippe Chédeville, *Cinquieme recueil de vaudevilles, menuets, contradanses, et autres airs* (Paris: Boivin & Le Clerc [173–]). Newberry Library, 6A 354. Reduction 0.38.

94. Jean Joseph Cassanea de Mondonville, *Le carnaval du Parnasse* (Paris: L'auteur [1749]). Newberry Library, VM 1520 M 74c. Reduction 0.41.

95. [Nicolas Médard Audinot], *Le tonnelier* (Paris: Le Clerc [1765?]). Newberry Library, VM 1500 A 912t 1765. Reduction 0.38.

96. Johann Franz Xaver Sterkel, *Sonate a 4 mains, oeuvre 15* (Paris: Boyer [c.1787]). Newberry Library, 8A 1033. Reduction 0.38.

156   97. M. Grénier, *Recueil des airs et duos des Deux tuteurs* [by Dalayrac] (Paris: L'auteur [178–]). Newberry Library, sVM 1508 D 13d. Reduction 0.38.

98. Daniel Steibelt, *Romeo et Juliette* (Paris: Boyer [1793]). Newberry Library, VM 1500 S 81r. Reduction 0.4.

99. Giovanni Paisiello, *Le bon maitre* (Paris: Sieber [1790?]). Newberry Library, VM 1500 P 14bo. Reduction 0.4.

100. Ignaz Joseph Pleyel, *Six nouvelles sonatines progressives, oeuvre 27* (Paris: L'auteur [c.1797]). Newberry Library, sVM 219 P 727s op.27. Reduction 0.38.

157   101. Johann Ladislaus Dussek, *Trois sonates et trois préludes, oeuvre 31* (Paris: A. Leduc [1805?]). Newberry Library, 8A 697. Reduction 0.38.

102. Louis Joseph Ferdinand Hérold, *Choeur des chasseurs, oeuvre 35* (Paris: Janet & Cotelle [c.1822]). Newberry Library, VM 3 H 56w. Reduction 0.37.

103. Anton Joseph Reicha, *Douze fugues pour le piano* (Paris: Imbault [180–]). Newberry Library, 6A 293. Reduction 0.38.

104. Friedrich Heinrich Himmel, *Trois sonates pour le piano forte, opera 16* (Paris: Imbault [c.1808]). Newberry Library, sVM 312 H 658s op.16 1808. Reduction 0.38.

159   105. John Field, *Trois rondeaux pour le piano forte* (Paris: Pacini [181–]). Newberry Library, 8A 726. Reduction 0.38.

106. Johann Baptist Cramer, *Air saxon avec variations* (Paris: Imbault [18——]). Newberry Library, 8A 661. Reduction 0.41.

107. Mr. Hus-Desforges, *Air de Joseph variè, oeuv. 40* (Paris: Pacini [c.1822]). Newberry Library, 8A 444. Reduction 0.38.

108. Jean-François Le Sueur, *Trois Te Deum* (Paris: Frey, 1829). Newberry Library, 6A 187. Reduction 0.4.

256

Pages	Figures
161	109. Giacomo Meyerbeer, *Robert le Diable* (Paris: Schlesinger [183–]). Newberry Library, 6A 273. Reduction 0.41.
	110. Daniel François Esprit Auber, *Le lac des fées* (Paris: Troupenas [1839?]). Newberry Library, VM 1503 A 88La. Reduction 0.4.
	111. Louis Hérold, *La clochette* (Paris: H. Lemoine [c.1855?]). Newberry Library, 5A 1374. Reduction 0.39.
	112. Henri Herz, *Fantaisie dramatique, op.89* (Paris: Schonenberger [183–]). Newberry Library, 8A 1177. Reduction 0.384.
163	113. Otto Nicolai, *Il templario* (Paris: Schlesinger [1840?]). Newberry Library, VM 1503 N 63t. Reduction 0.34.
	114. Théodore Labarre, *Album 1842.* (Paris: Troupenas [1842]). Newberry Library, VM 1620 L 113a 1842. Reduction 0.42.
	115. Alexander Ernst Fesca, *2e grand quatuor, op.28* (Paris: Richault [184–?]). Newberry Library, VM 412 F 41q2. Reduction 0.38.
164	116. Daniel François Esprit Auber, *Haydée, ou Le secret* (Paris: Troupenas [1850?]). Newberry Library, VM 1503 A 88h. Reduction 0.42.
	117. Giacomo Meyerbeer, *Marguerita d'Anjou* (Paris: Brandus [c.1850]). Newberry Library, VM 1503 M 61m. Reduction 0.4.
	118. Antonin Guillot, *Album* (Paris: Richault [1850]). Newberry Library, VM 1620 G 96a. Reduction 0.39.
166	119. Jean Michel Pfeiffer, *La bambina al cembalo* 2. ed. (Venice: Zatta [c.1790]). Newberry Library, 7Q 131. Reduction 0.42.
	120. Pasquale Cafaro, *Stabat Mater* (Naples 1785). Newberry Library, VM 2021 C 129s. Reduction 0.42.
	121. Adolf von Henselt, *12 études caractéristiques de concert, op.2* (Naples: Girard [18––]). Newberry Library, VMT 241 H 52e. Reduction 0.36.
169	122. Giovanni Pacini, *Ivanhoe* (Milan: Ricordi [1832]). Newberry Library, VM 1503 P 11i. Reduction 0.34.
	123. Carlo Pedrotti, *Tutti in maschera* (Milan: G. Ricordi [1856?]). Newberry Library, 7Q 69. Reduction 0.34.
	124. Giuseppe Mercadante, *Leonora* (Milan: Lucca [1844?]). Newberry Library, VM 1503 M 55L. Reduction 0.35.
171	125. Bonifazio Asioli, *Trattato di armonia* (Milan: Ricordi [1813]). Newberry Library, fV 54 .053. Reduction 0.31.
	126. Bonifazio Asioli, *Trattato di armonia* (Milan: Ricordi [1836?]). Newberry Library, fV .054. Reduction 0.31.
172	127. Friedrich Kunzen, *Das Halleluja der Schöpfung* (Zurich: Nägeli, [1800]). Newberry Library, VM 2000 K 97h. Reduction 0.35.
	128. Johann Sebastian Bach, *Das wohltemperirte Clavier* (Zurich: Nägeli [1801]). Newberry Library, Case VMT 247 B 11w 1801a. Reduction 0.34.
	129. Václav Tomašek, *Sonate & rondeau pour le piano forte* (Zurich: Nägeli [180–]). Newberry Library, 8A 952. Reduction 0.34.

Pages	Figures

130. Heinrich Marschner, *Fünf gesänge für drei weibliche stimmen, op.188* (Winterthur: Rieter-Biedermann [c.1860]). Newberry Library, VM 1551 M 36f. Reduction 0.34.

174   131. Johann Rudolf Zumsteeg, *Hagars Klage in der Wüste Bersaba* (Leipzig: Breitkopf & Härtel [c.1810]). Newberry Library, sVM 1621 Z 95h. Reduction 0.33.

132. Giuseppe Sarti, *Lob sey dem allerhöchsten Gott!* (Leipzig: Breitkopf & Härtel [1813]). Newberry Library, 7Q 51. Reduction 0.33.

133. Michael Haydn, *Tenebrae* (Leipzig: Breitkopf & Härtel [1826]). Newberry Library, sVM 2078 .G5 H 416t. Reduction 0.33.

177   134. John Field, *Quatrième concerto pour le pianoforte* (Leipzig: Breitkopf & Härtel [1816?]). Newberry Library, VM 1011 F 45c4. Reduction 0.36.

135. Robert Schumann, *Carnaval, oeuv. 9* (Leipzig: Breitkopf & Härtel [1837]). Newberry Library, 8A 1189. Reduction 0.35.

136. Niels Gade, *Sonate für pianoforte und violine, op.21* (Leipzig: Breitkopf & Härtel [1850]). Newberry Library, sVM 219 G 12s2. Reduction 0.35.

137. Anton Leoni Kuhn, *Trois sonates, oeuvre II.* (Mannheim: Götz [c.1785]). Newberry Library, 6A 342. Reduction 0.35.

178   138. [Benedict Schack], *Der dumme Gärtner, fürs Clavier gesetzt von C.G. Neefe* (Bonn: Simrock [1794?]). Newberry Library, VM 1503 S 29a. Reduction 0.36.

139. Carl Czerny, *Rondeau brillant sur des walses favorites de Jos. Lanner, op.491* (Bonn: Simrock [1839?]). Newberry Library, 8A 1353. Reduction 0.36.

140. Walter von Goethe, *Slavische Bilder, op.22, 2tes Heft.* (Bonn: Simrock [1851]). Newberry Library, 8A 741. Reduction 0.36.

179   141. Johann Ladislaus Dussek, *Six sonates, oeuvre 28* (Bonn: Simrock [1803?]). Newberry Library, 8A 695. Reduction 0.39.

142. John Field, *Rondeau pour le piano forte . . . No. III* (Bonn: Simrock [1818?]). Newberry Library, 8A 417. Reduction 0.39.

143. Ludwig van Beethoven, *Sonates pour le piano . . . Édition revue . . . par Ch. Czerny* (Bonn: Simrock [185—]). Newberry Library, 8A 1459. Reduction 0.39.

181   144. Johann Baptist Wanhal, *Six sonates, oeuvre I* (Offenbach: André [1784?]). Newberry Library, sVM 23 W 24s. Reduction 0.36.

145. Daniel Steibelt, *Combat naval, oeuvre 36.* "Seconde Ed." (Offenbach: André [1807?]). Newberry Library, 8A 1180. Reduction 0.36.

146. John Field, *Rondeau du 2me Concert* (Offenbach: André [1820]). Newberry Library, 8A 397. Reduction 0.35.

183   147. Hans von Aufsess, *Fünf Walzer, op.4* (Munich: Falter [18——?]). Newberry Library, 8A 409. Reduction 0.36.

148. Wilhelm Speyer, *Die Stille, 46tes Werk* (Mainz: Schott [1843?]). Newberry Library, 8A 530. Reduction 0.36.

149. Franz Liszt, *Années de pèlerinage, 1. année* (Mainz: Schott [1855]). Newberry Library, 6A 461. Reduction 0.36.

185   150. Johann Sebastian Bach, *Exercises pour le clavecin* (Vienna: Hoffmeister; Leipzig: Bureau de musique [1801]). Newberry Library, sVM 24 B 11p no.1 1801. Reduction 0.36.

Pages   *Figures*

194. János Spech, *Hat magyar dal, [op.30]* (Pest: Miller [182—]). Newberry Library, 8A 220. Reduction 0.36.

195. János Kirch, *A' markotánosnö* (Pesten: Rózsavölgyi és Társa, [185—?]). Newberry Library, 8A 852. Reduction 0.36.

196. Ignácz Frank, *Apám nótája* (Pesten: Rözsavölgyi és Társa 1863). Newberry Library, 8A 857. Reduction 0.36.

212   197. *Wybór pięknych dziel muzycznych y pieśni polskich, No.1* (Warsaw: [Sztycharnia nut Elsnera], 1803). Warsaw, Biblioteka Narodowa, mf. 13058.

198. Józef Cybulski, *Trois polonaises pour le clavecin ou piano-forte* (Warsaw: The Author [1805/6]). Warsaw: Biblioteka Narodowa, mf. 27657.

199. Karol Kurpiński, *Zasady muzyki na klawikord* (Warsaw: A. Brzeziny i Komp. 1829). Warsaw: Biblioteka Narodowa, mf. 16226.

215   200. *Terpsychora czyli zbiór naynowszych i naybarodziey ulubionych w Towarzystwach Warsazwskich rozmaitych tanców na pianoforte, No.8* (Warsaw: Letronne, 1821). Warsaw: Biblioteka Narodowa, Mus.II.20865.

201. Antoni Teichmann, *Wenecya, Barkarola do śpiewu z towarzyszeniem fortepianu* (Warsaw: G. Sennewald [c.1845]). Warsaw: Biblioteka Narodowa, Mus.II.20857.

202. Maxymilian Einert, *La Mode; Cinq contredanses pour le piano-forte* (Warsaw: G. Sennewald [c.1845]). Warsaw: Biblioteka Narodowa, Mus.II.17825.

217   203. Karol Kurpiński, *Wyklad systematyczny zasad muzyki na klawikord* (Warsaw: F. Klukowski [1818]). Warsaw: Biblioteka Narodowa, mf. 31942.

204. Antoni Léskiewicz, *Polonaise pour le piano-forte* (Warsaw: Magnus [c.1829]). Warsaw: Biblioteka Narodowa, B.J.576.III.Mus.

205. Jósef Achtel, *Z szczerego serca* (Warsaw: Spiess [c.1845]). Warsaw: Biblioteka Narodowa, Mus.II.17866.

221   206. C. Schall, *Musiken til Balletten Sigrid* ([Copenhagen 180—]). Newberry Library, 7Q 254. Reduction 0.36.

207. C.E.F. Weyse, *XXIV eccossaises pour le pianoforte* (Copenhagen: Lose [1823]). Newberry Library, 8A 1551. Reduction 0.36.

208. C.E.F. Weyse, *Huit études pour le piano forte, oeuvre 51* (Copenhagen: Lose [1831]). Newberry Library, 8A 1552. Reduction 0.36.

222   209. J.A.P. Schulz, *Maria og Johannes; Et Passions-Oratorium* (Copenhagen: Sønnichsen, 1789). Newberry Library, 7Q 261. Reduction 0.37.

210. Joseph Haydn, *Sinfonie af Haydn lämpad för claver af Palm* ([n.p.] 1791). Newberry Library, sVM 35 H 41s62. Reduction 0.4.

211. Johann Berwald, *Danse suédoise* (Stockholm: Müller [182—]). Newberry Library, 8A 1550. Reduction 0.4.

226   212. Adolf von Henselt, *Ballade pour le piano, op.31* (St. Pétersbourg: Stellowsky [185—?]). Newberry Library, 8A 739. Reduction 0.39.

213. L. Petrov, *Pogadai-ka mnie starushka; Air bohêmien-russe, op.131* (St. Petersbourg: Krug [186—?]). Newberry Library, 8A 965. Reduction 0.39.

228   214. *How Cheerful Along the Gay Mead.* (Philadelphia: Carr [179—]). Newberry Library, Driscoll Collection. Reduction 0.36.

261

Index to Citations

A list of musical compositions, editions of which are cited as examples in the text (with reference to the page number), or reproduced as Figures (see the List of Illustrations, pp. 251–63).

View of the interior of the Publishers Great Piano & Music Establishment

Figure 242: INTERIOR OF THE HORACE WATERS "MUSIC SALOON" IN NEW YORK, 1855.